CRYPTOCURRENCY FOR BEGINNERS

Your Essential Guide to Blockchain, Investments, Bitcoin and the Future of Finance.

Max Davidson

Cryptocurrency for Beginners
© Copyright 2024 All rights reserved.
Written by Max Davidson

Overview

a. The Introduction of the Author

Greetings and salutations from "Cryptocurrency for Beginners"! My name is Max Davidson, and I'm the author of this tutorial, which is intended especially for people who are just starting out with cryptocurrencies. I'll serve as your guide as you easily navigate the fascinating world of Bitcoin and the related technologies throughout this book.

There's a chance you're thinking, "Bitcoin? Cryptocurrencies? It all sounds a bit too complicated for me." Don't worry, this book is designed to make these theoretically difficult ideas understandable to everyone. Here you'll find concise answers to all of your queries, regardless of your level of experience in the field.

My commitment to you is to deliver knowledge that is precise, substantiated, and, most all, comprehensible. The intention is for your experience with Bitcoin and cryptocurrencies to be both entertaining and enlightening. Our goal is to demystify and simplify this intriguing topic for you.

So, without further ado, let's dive right into the Bitcoin world!

b. A succinct justification for the book's beginner-friendly status

"Why should I pick up 'Cryptocurrency for Beginners'?" you may be asking yourself. Allow me to explain. This book is specifically designed for those who are just beginning to dabble in the wide world of cryptocurrency. This is why it's the ideal place to start:

The key is simplicity: We recognize that the world of Bitcoin can initially seem overwhelming. This book was written with simplicity in mind because of this. We ensure that you won't feel overwhelmed by simplifying difficult subjects into language that is easy to understand.

No Past Experience Necessary: This book is for everyone, regardless of financial expertise or lack thereof. Assuming you have no prior knowledge, we begin at the beginning and walk you through each step of the essentials.

Simple and Direct: Ignore technical jargon and nonsense. " Cryptocurrency for Beginners " offers concise explanations free of needless complication. Because each chapter is intended to be brief, reading it will be easy and entertaining.

Realistic Perspectives: We don't only bombard you with data. The book is brimming with useful advice, real-world examples, and suggestions that you can put to use right away. It's not only about knowing; it's about having the ability to comfortably traverse the bitcoin world.

Demystifying Cryptocurrencies: Although they may appear mysterious, have no fear! The decoder ring is inside this book. We cut through the complexity, dispel myths, and provide you a strong basis on which to base your judgments.

'Cryptocurrency for Beginners' is therefore your go-to resource if you're a newbie ready to solve the puzzles around Bitcoin and cryptocurrencies. Together, let's take this adventure one easy step at a time.

Bitcoin's past

a. genesis and production

Let's explore the intriguing beginnings of Bitcoin, a virtual money that surfaced out of nowhere and completely changed the financial landscape. The narrative starts with an enigmatic character known as Satoshi Nakamoto, whose real identity is still a mystery.

The Emmy-winning Satoshi Nakamoto in 2008, Nakamoto published a whitepaper titled "Bitcoin: A Peer-to-Peer Electronic Cash System." Although he worked under a pseudonym, Nakamoto is still unknown, but his innovative idea for Bitcoin ignited a financial revolution.

Genesis Block: The Start of a New Era Nakamoto officially created Bitcoin in January 2009 when he mined the first block of the blockchain, known as "Genesis Block" or "Block 0." This momentous event brought the cryptocurrency to life. A moving message that alluded to the headlines of the day was embedded in the Coinbase parameter of this block: "The Times 03/Jan/2009 Chancellor on brink of second bailout for banks."

Decentralization and the Power of Open Source: The decentralized design of Bitcoin sets it different. Bitcoin runs on a peer-to-peer network, in contrast to conventional currencies that are managed by centralized organizations. Because the software is open-source, anyone can access and modify its code, encouraging transparency and teamwork.

The Halving: Sculpting Scarcity In order to control the amount of Bitcoin that is available, Nakamoto introduced a ground-breaking technique called "halving." This means that the reward that miners get for confirming transactions is reduced by half around every four years. With a limited supply of 21 million bitcoins, this deliberate scarcity contributes to the distinctive economic dynamics of the cryptocurrency.

The path from Nakamoto's groundbreaking whitepaper to the development of the Genesis Block established the foundation for a digital currency that goes against traditional ideas of money. We'll walk through the significant occasions and turning points that made Bitcoin into the adaptable and revolutionary commodity it is today in the upcoming chapters.

b. Changes over time

Tracing the history of Bitcoin reveals an incredible path characterized by acceptance hurdles, technological improvements, and increasing international awareness.

Early on: The Pioneer Years Bitcoin functioned rather covertly in its early years. Its ability to upend established banking systems and guarantee financial sovereignty drew early adopters and enthusiasts. Around this time, a small group of tech-savvy people who were attracted to the novel idea of a decentralized digital currency began to take an interest in Bitcoin.

Market Adoption - Bitcoin's Increase in Value During its early years, the value of Bitcoin saw considerable swings. The cryptocurrency steadily gained pace and attracted interest from investors looking for an alternative store of value in spite of skepticism and volatility. The notorious incident that occurred in 2011 on the Silk Road, an online bazaar for illegal items, helped bring Bitcoin even more notoriety.

Maturity and Acceptance: Over time, Bitcoin evolved into a respectable financial asset by overcoming legislative obstacles and distrust. Users may now use Bitcoin to make real-world purchases thanks to its acceptance by a growing number of companies and retailers, which enhanced its legitimacy. This period of time was crucial because it saw the evolution of Bitcoin from an innovative idea to a widely accepted form of payment.

Institutional Involvement: This marked the beginning of a new phase in the development of Bitcoin. A sense of legitimacy was introduced by well-known sponsorships, investments, and the involvement of financial institutions in the bitcoin industry. Because institutional investors saw Bitcoin as a hedge against economic risks, its reputation as "digital gold" grew.

Technical Improvements: In order to solve scalability and transaction speed difficulties, significant advancements were made to the underlying technology of Bitcoin through the use of Segregated Witness and Lightning Network. Segregated Witness (SegWit) was implemented, and the Lightning Network was created with the goal of increasing transaction efficiency and making Bitcoin more useful for regular transactions.

Worldwide Acknowledgment and Regulation Managing the intricate web of international laws was another aspect of Bitcoin's development. Different nations reacted to cryptocurrencies in different ways: some adopted them, while others put strict restrictions on them. But this widespread acceptance also highlighted Bitcoin's importance as a game-changing innovation in the financial industry.

It's clear from examining Bitcoin's development over time that it has been resilient, flexible, and constantly seeking greater acceptance and understanding. We'll continue to piece together the history of Bitcoin in the upcoming chapters by looking at the factors that have formed it thus far and will likely continue to do so.

C. Important periods in the Bitcoin history

The story of Bitcoin is interspersed with critical events that have molded its course, impacted public opinion, and cemented its standing as a disruptive force in the financial industry.

1. Pizza Day: May 22, 2010: The well-known "Pizza Day" occurred on May 22, 2010, and it is one of the first known Bitcoin transactions. Laszlo Hanyecz, a programmer, exchanged 10,000 bitcoins for a pair of pizzas. Though with a value that is now considered extraordinary, this event was the first time that Bitcoin was used as a means of exchange in the real world.

2. October 2, 2013 saw the closure of the notorious dark web marketplace Silk Road, which was a major influence in the early development of Bitcoin. When law enforcement shut it down in 2013, it highlighted Bitcoin's link to illegal activity and sparked debates about potential regulatory ramifications.

3. February 24, 2014: Mt. Gox Collapsed: Once the biggest Bitcoin exchange, Mt. Gox's 2014 collapse brought about by a significant hack and subsequent insolvency had far-reaching effects. It brought attention to the shortcomings of centralized exchanges and led to calls for tighter security measures in the bitcoin space.

4. Events of Bitcoin Halving The halving, which is a special method of supply, takes place about every four years. The first halved happened in 2012, and there were more halvings in 2016 and 2020. The pace at which new bitcoins are created is lowered

during these halving events, which are significant events that affect Bitcoin's scarcity and have historically been linked to price rises.

5. Mainstream Acceptance - 2017 Due to a significant increase in Bitcoin's value, the year 2017 saw a rise in its popularity. The rapid rise of Bitcoin was facilitated by growing institutional interest, more media attention, and the introduction of Bitcoin futures on key exchanges. This time frame was crucial in establishing Bitcoin as a respectable asset class.

6. Bull Run of 2020–2021: During this period of time, which started in late 2020 and continued into 2021, Bitcoin reached all-time highs. Institutional investments, rising individual investor interest, and increased awareness of Bitcoin as an inflation hedge all contributed to this boom.

7. September 7, 2021: El Salvador became the first government to officially recognize Bitcoin as legal cash. This was a landmark day in the country's history. This ruling sparked debates regarding the place of cryptocurrencies in national economies and raised awareness of Bitcoin's possible application in regular transactions on a worldwide scale.

8. Sustained Regulations Bitcoin has been greatly impacted by ongoing regulations around the world. Different nations have taken different stances; some have welcomed it while others have put tight restrictions in place. The way that regulations are changing around the world is still influencing how people view and use bitcoin.

These significant events in Bitcoin's history represent turning points in the company's development from an innovative idea to a powerful force in the financial industry. We learn more about the elements that have contributed to Bitcoin's rise to fame as we examine these instances.

Blockchain: The Fundamental Technology

a. A brief explanation of blockchain

Blockchain technology is the groundwork for several other cryptocurrencies, including Bitcoin. Let's simplify the basic premise underlying a blockchain in order to demystify this concept.

The Decentralized Ledger at the Heart of Blockchain

Imagine a record-keeping system, such as a digital ledger, that isn't governed by a single organization, such as a government or bank. Rather, it is decentralized, which means that no single entity has total control over it. A blockchain's essential component is this decentralized ledger.

Blocks in the Chain: Transparency Builds Trust

Let's now visualize this digital ledger as a block chain. A list of transactions—digital data detailing who sent and received cryptocurrency—is included in every block. Blockchain is distinct because each new block is connected to the one before it by means of a chain once it has been filled with transactions. All transactions are recorded in a chronological and immutable manner thanks to the chaining of blocks.

Security and Decentralization: The Influence of Consensus

How new transactions are added to the chain is where the magic happens. Blockchain relies on a consensus method as opposed to a central authority. This implies that a transaction cannot be added to the ledger unless a network of computers, known as nodes, concur that it is valid. Due to the decentralized consensus, security and transparency are guaranteed, making it very difficult for information to be manipulated.

Using Cryptography to Secure the Chain

Advanced cryptographic algorithms are used by blockchain to protect the integrity of each block. A hash is a special code that is created for every block based on the data in that block. The hash updates to notify the network of any attempted tampering if someone tries to change the data in a block. The entire chain is further protected by this cryptographic security.

Blockchain's promise of being trustworthy and unchangeable

To put it briefly, a blockchain is a network of linked, decentralized blocks, each of which has a safe record of transactions. Because of its strength in transparency, security, and immutability, this technology is dependable not just for cryptocurrencies but also for a wide range of applications across industries. We'll examine how blockchain technology transcends banking and influences value and trust exchange in the digital era as we go deeper into the subject.

b. How Blockchain Operates

After learning the fundamentals of blockchain, let's examine how this cutting-edge technology functions internally and discover how it keeps a safe and open record.

1. Transaction Initiation: When a participant starts a transaction on a blockchain, it starts its journey. This participant could be an individual, an organization, or even a smart contract, which is an automated software that, in the event that certain circumstances are satisfied, carries out predetermined actions.

2. Verification through Nodes: A transaction is sent out to a network of computers called nodes as soon as it is started. These nodes are essential components of the blockchain network. They verify that the transaction complies with network regulations and that the sender possesses the required funds or authority.

3. Forming a Block: After a transaction has been validated, it is gathered into a block. A predetermined number of transactions and a reference to the preceding block via its distinct hash are usually included in each block. The distinctive chain formation is produced by the connections between the components.

4. Consensus Mechanism: A consensus between the nodes is required in order to add a block to the blockchain. To reach consensus, a variety of consensus techniques are used, including Proof of Work (PoW) and Proof of Stake (PoS). Whereas nodes with a larger stake in the network are given preference in PoS,

nodes compete to solve challenging mathematical puzzles in PoW.

5. Adding the Block to the Chain: The new block is appended to the current blockchain upon the achievement of a consensus. Confirmation is the step that makes sure the transaction is now a permanent and unchangeable part of the ledger.

6. Cryptographic Security: Cryptographic hash functions are used to strengthen the integrity of every block. A mathematical procedure is used to a block's contents to produce a unique hash. A completely different hash would be produced by any modification to the block's contents, warning the network of any possible tampering.

7. Distributed Ledger: The decentralized nature of blockchain is one of its main advantages. Every node in the network has a copy of the whole blockchain. This distributed ledger makes guarantee that data is safe and available on other nodes, even in the event that one node malfunctions or is compromised.

8. Immutability and Transparency: A block is almost impossible to change once it is added to the blockchain. The distributed ledger, cryptographic security, and decentralized consensus process all add to the data's immutability. Transparency is further ensured by allowing everyone on the network to view the complete transaction history.

The potential of blockchain as a reliable, decentralized system for transaction recording and verification becomes clear when one understands how it operates. The forthcoming parts will delve into the manifold uses of blockchain technology that extend beyond cryptocurrencies, demonstrating its revolutionary influence on an array of industries.

C. Blockchain's Security and Transparency

Decentralization, consensus, and cryptographic security are the cornerstones of blockchain technology, and they play a major role in the exceptional security and transparency qualities of the system. Let's examine how these components cooperate to protect data and keep an open ledger that is available to everyone.

1. Decentralization: A fundamental component of blockchain security is its decentralized structure. Conventional systems are susceptible to manipulation or attacks because they frequently depend on a single point of control. Blockchain, on the other hand, runs on a global network of nodes. Since every node has a copy of the whole blockchain, no one entity is able to hold all the power. Because of the network's decentralized architecture, it is very difficult for malevolent actors to compromise the entire system.

2. Consensus method: One of the most important aspects of improving security is the consensus method that blockchain networks use. All nodes in the chain must concur that the proposed transactions are legitimate before a new block is appended to the chain. This agreement guarantees that illegal or fraudulent transactions are rejected and is attained by consensus

methods like as Proof of Work (PoW) or Proof of Stake (PoS). The unanimity criterion serves as a strong deterrent to harmful activity on the network.

3. Blockchain uses cutting-edge cryptography techniques to safeguard the confidentiality and integrity of data. Every block has a distinct hash, which is a complicated code produced depending on the data in that block. Any attempt to change the content of the block would produce a whole new hash, alerting the network to possible manipulation right away. This cryptographic security protects against unwanted access in addition to guaranteeing the blockchain's immutability.

4. Distributed Ledger: Security and transparency are greatly enhanced by the distributed ledger design. The possibility of a single point of failure is reduced because each node has a copy of the whole blockchain stored on it. Because the network is decentralized, much of it is protected even in the event that one node is compromised. The blockchain is protected against assaults and data loss thanks to its redundancy.

5. Immutability: A block is essentially unchangeable once it is added to the blockchain. The distributed ledger, decentralized consensus, and cryptographic hashing work together to make it difficult to change past transactions. An essential component is immutability, which creates an unalterable and trustworthy record of transactions and promotes participant trust.

6. Transparency: The public and easily available ledger of blockchain is the foundation of its transparency. The complete

transaction history, from the genesis block to the most recent one, is visible to everyone on the network. In addition to fostering trust, this transparency makes it possible to verify transactions in real time. By enabling participants to independently confirm the blockchain's integrity, fraud can be less likely to occur and accountability can be increased.

Essentially, blockchain's transparency and security are integrated to provide a strong and reliable framework for transaction recording and verification. As we investigate deeper, we'll see how these characteristics affect sectors like supply chain management, healthcare, and more, in addition to cryptocurrency applications.

Additional Well-Known Cryptocurrencies

a. Introductory discussion of cryptocurrencies such as Litecoin, Ethereum, and Ripple.

Overview of Additional Well-Known Cryptocurrencies

Although Bitcoin is regarded as the forerunner of cryptocurrencies, there is still much to be discovered about the complex digital terrain. A plethora of alternative cryptocurrencies, also known as altcoins, have surfaced, each with its distinct features and applications. Beyond Bitcoin, let's examine a few notable participants in the cryptocurrency market.

1. Ethereum (ETH): Decentralized Applications (DApps) and Smart Contracts: Ethereum, which is sometimes regarded as the second-largest cryptocurrency by market capitalization, is capable of more than just transferring money. Ethereum, which was founded in 2015 by Vitalik Buterin, popularized the idea of smart contracts, which are self-executing agreements with explicit language included in the code. This feature opens up a wide range of possibilities beyond simple transactions by allowing the development of decentralized applications (DApps) that function without centralized control.

2. Ripple (XRP): Enabling Cross-Border Payments Through the provision of faster and more affordable cross-border payment

services, Ripple seeks to completely transform the established banking industry. In contrast to other cryptocurrencies, Ripple runs on a centralized network and has alliances with many international financial institutions. By serving as a conduit between various fiat currencies, the XRP cryptocurrency expedites cross-border transactions and shortens settlement times.

3. Litecoin (LTC): Silver to Bitcoin's Gold Often called the "silver to Bitcoin's gold," Charlie Lee founded the cryptocurrency in 2011. While it is quite similar to Bitcoin, it differs from it in that it uses a different hashing algorithm and has faster block creation times. Litecoin is intended to preserve the fundamental ideas of decentralization while offering a faster and more scalable substitute for routine transactions.

4. Cardano (ADA): Aiming for Sustainability and Scalability Charles Hoskinson, an Ethereum co-founder, founded Cardano with an emphasis on interoperability, scalability, and sustainability. Cardano, which is renowned for its research-driven methodology, wants to build a blockchain network that is safe and long-lasting. It allows for more flexibility and scalability by breaking up its development into discrete levels and isolating the ledger of accounts from the rationale behind value movements.

5. Polkadot (DOT): Enabling Interoperability amongst Blockchains: Dr. Gavin Wood, an Ethereum co-founder, launched Polkadot, which focuses on interoperability, or the capacity of several blockchains to exchange data and communicate with one another. It seeks to establish a web in which we control the

ownership of our data and decide where and how it is kept. The Polkadot network's native currency is the DOT coin.

6. Fueling the Binance Ecosystem, Binance Coin (BNB) was first introduced as an ERC-20 token on the Ethereum network. It has subsequently moved to Binance Chain, Binance's proprietary blockchain. BNB is used for a variety of purposes on the Binance exchange, including token sales on the Binance Launchpad and payment of transaction fees. As one of the most popular utility tokens in the cryptocurrency market, it sticks out.

These are only a handful of the several cryptocurrency variations that have emerged since the creation of Bitcoin. Each adds to the expanding and dynamic ecosystem of digital currencies with its own special qualities and functions. We'll examine their unique features and how they've broadened the scope of possibilities in the blockchain world as we continue to investigate.

b. Important Distinctions Between Other Cryptocurrencies and Bitcoin

Although Bitcoin opened the door for the world of cryptocurrencies, a wide range of other digital assets are now part of the scene. The following are some salient features that distinguish Bitcoin from other cryptocurrencies:

1. Goal and Instance of Use:

Bitcoin (BTC): Originally intended to be a decentralized digital currency, peer-to-peer transactions and value storage are the main applications for Bitcoin. It functions as an international, unrestricted means of communication.

Ethereum (ETH): Ethereum is a platform that focuses on decentralized apps (DApps) and smart contracts rather than just currency. Its blockchain introduces programmable capability beyond transactions, enabling developers to design a variety of applications.

2. Mechanism of Consensus:

Bitcoin (BTC): In order to confirm transactions and add new blocks to the blockchain, miners compete to solve challenging mathematical puzzles as part of the Proof of Work (PoW) consensus mechanism.

Cardano (ADA): Cardano makes use of the Ouroboros PoS (Proof of Stake) consensus method, which increases the likelihood that validators with a larger network stake will be selected to produce new blocks. The goal of this method is to use less energy than PoW.

3. Quickness and Expandability:

Litecoin (LTC): Compared to Bitcoin, Litecoin is frequently praised for having faster block creation times. Because of the faster transaction confirmations made possible by the lower block time, it is more suited for daily transactions.

Polkadot (DOT): Polkadot aims to connect several blockchains with an emphasis on interoperability and scalability. Increased transaction throughput and improved scalability across linked chains are made possible by its design.

4. Model of Governance:

Bitcoin (BTC): Bitcoin relies on user, developer, and miner consensus to decide on protocol changes. It is governed by a decentralized, community-driven paradigm.

Cardano (ADA): ADA holders can take part in choices about network upgrades thanks to Cardano's governance model, which includes a treasury system and voting procedures.

5. Total Supply and Rate of Emissions:

Bitcoin (BTC): The mining process creates new bitcoins, which have a limited supply of 21 million. Its perceived store of worth is partly attributed to this scarcity.

Ethereum (ETH): With the release of Ethereum 2.0, Ethereum intends to use a Proof of Stake consensus mechanism in addition to a regulated issuance rate. Originally, Ethereum had an unbounded supply.

6. Method of Development:

Bitcoin (BTC): Bitcoin is renowned for its cautious development methodology, emphasizing stability and security. Modifications to the protocol frequently necessitate widespread community agreement.

Ripple (XRP): Ripple uses a more centralized business model, with a single organization managing the creation of its XRP Ledger. Although this method speeds up decision-making, it has come under fire for departing from the decentralized spirit of many cryptocurrencies.

Comprehending these salient distinctions underscores the adaptability inherent in the bitcoin landscape. Every digital asset has a special set of advantages that meet different user requirements and increase the potential of blockchain technology. We'll keep discovering the unique qualities of other cryptocurrencies and their contributions to the changing cryptocurrency scene as we investigate deeper.

Blockchain Applications

a. Smart Contracts: Blockchain-Based Transformative Automation

The idea of smart contracts is one of the revolutionary uses of blockchain technology that has helped it advance beyond cryptocurrency. Self-executing contracts, or smart contracts, have their terms encoded directly into the code. Let's explore how smart contracts are revolutionary and how they are changing conventional contractual procedures.

1. Smart Contracts: What Are They? Smart contracts are digital contracts made to carry out, automate, or enforce a contract's provisions without the use of middlemen. They function according to the tenets of blockchain, making use of its tamper-resistant and decentralized characteristics to guarantee security and transparency in contractual agreements.

2. The Operation of Smart Contracts:

Coding the Agreement: A smart contract is created by converting a contract's terms and conditions into code. The terms of the contract will automatically execute when the predefined rules and conditions in this code are met.

Decentralized Execution: Because smart contracts operate on blockchain networks, their execution is dispersed amongst nodes and is decentralized. This increases efficiency and lowers expenses by doing away with the requirement for a central authority to supervise or enforce the contract.

3. Important attributes:

Trustless Execution: Smart contracts function according to the trustless concept, which permits parties to enter into agreements without requiring mutual trust. The terms are enforced by the code itself, removing any possibility of fraud or manipulation.

Transparency: A smart contract's whole history is transparent and unchangeable since it records all of its activities and transactions on the blockchain. Accountability is increased when participants are able to follow the contract's whole lifecycle.

4. Practical Uses:

Financial Services: From executing intricate financial instruments to enabling decentralized lending and borrowing platforms, smart contracts automate a range of financial operations.

Supply Chain Management: Smart contracts can reduce fraud and inefficiencies in supply chains by tracking the flow of items, automatically initiating payments, and enforcing compliance with predetermined criteria.

Real Estate Transactions: By automating the transfer of property ownership, managing payments, and guaranteeing compliance with contractual requirements, smart contracts simplify real estate transactions.

Insurance Claims Processing: By automating insurance claim procedures, smart contracts can speed up the approval and payment of claims in accordance with predetermined guidelines, increase transparency, and shorten processing times.

5. Obstacles & Things to Think About:

Code Vulnerabilities: The security of smart contracts depends on the code in which they are built. Because code vulnerabilities can result in exploitations, thorough code audits are crucial.

Legal Recognition: Although smart contracts and blockchain provide technological answers, legal frameworks are still lagging behind. Ensuring legal enforceability and recognition is a continuous challenge.

Smart contracts herald a paradigm shift in the creation, performance, and enforcement of contracts. Their capacity to automate complicated procedures without the need for middlemen creates new opportunities for a variety of businesses, promoting efficiency, openness, and confidence in the digital age. We will find more applications that make use of blockchain technology as we continue our exploration.

b. Supply Chain Management: Using Blockchain to Revive Transparency and Efficiency

Blockchain technology has become a potent instrument in supply chain management, providing revolutionary answers to enduring problems. Let's examine how supply chain management and optimization are being transformed by blockchain.

1. The Complicated Supply Chain Environment:

Visibility and Complexity: The absence of real-time visibility in traditional supply chains frequently results in inefficiencies, delays, and challenges monitoring the flow of commodities through several phases.

Trust issues: Traditional techniques may not be transparent, which makes it difficult to verify the validity and provenance of products. Trust is vital in supply chain interactions.

2. Blockchain Technology in the Logistics Industry:

Decentralized Ledger: Every transaction and movement of products is recorded in an immutable, decentralized ledger that is made possible by blockchain technology. All authorized parties in the supply chain network have access to this ledger.

Enhanced Transparency: Participants are able to follow a product's whole path from the point of origin to the final customer. Because of this transparency, there is a lower chance of fraud, counterfeiting, and unapproved supply chain changes.

Smart Contracts for Automation: Smart contracts can be used to automate a number of supply chain operations, such as order fulfillment, payment settlement, and compliance checks. This speeds up transaction processing, minimizes errors, and decreases the need for manual intervention.

3. Important Uses:

Provenance tracking: Blockchain makes it possible to keep a thorough record of a product's beginning and path. Participants can confirm the legitimacy and caliber of products all the way from the raw components to the final result.

Diminishing Counterfeiting: The likelihood of fake goods infiltrating the supply chain is reduced by blockchain's openness. Businesses and consumers alike can have faith in the authenticity of the goods they buy.

Process Streamlining: Customs clearance, invoicing, payment settlements, and other supply chain operations are all made more efficient by automation using smart contracts. This lowers operating expenses, paperwork, and delays.

Real-time Visibility: The location and status of products in transit may be seen in real-time thanks to blockchain technology. Better forecasting, proactive problem solving, and decision-making are made possible by this visibility.

4. Adoption by Industry and Success Stories:

Food Safety: To improve traceability, the food business has utilized blockchain technology. Retail behemoths employ blockchain technology to locate tainted product sources fast, facilitating prompt product recalls and averting serious health problems.

Pharmaceuticals: To stop the spread of fake medications, the pharmaceutical sector uses blockchain technology. Patients are provided with genuine and safe products by guaranteeing the authenticity of medications.

Automotive: By recording the manufacture and delivery of automotive components, blockchain lowers the possibility of errors and improves overall quality control.

5. Overcoming Obstacles:

Integration with Current Systems: It can be difficult to integrate blockchain technology with current supply chain management systems. collaboration between technology providers and stakeholders is necessary for successful implementation.

Scalability: Ensuring the scalability of blockchain networks becomes essential as supply chains contain a number of transactions. The goal of ongoing blockchain technology developments is to solve scalability issues.

To put it briefly, supply chain management may improve efficiency, transparency, and traceability by utilizing blockchain technology. In the ever-changing world of supply chain operations, we should expect even more innovation and acceptance as sectors continue to see its potential.

C. Digital Identity: Giving People Safe, Transportable Identities

The idea of digital identity is becoming more and more popular in the era of digital transformation as a way to solve problems with identity verification, privacy, and security. Blockchain technology gives users more protection and control over their personal data by establishing a strong framework for managing digital identities.

1. Conventional Identity Systems' Challenge:

Silos and Fragmentation: Traditional identification systems frequently produce siloed, fragmented databases that are kept up to date by different organizations, which can result in security risks and inefficiencies.

Privacy Concerns: Since personal information is centralized in one place and is therefore a desirable target for malevolent actors, centralized identity systems may put users at risk for privacy violations.

2. Digital identity and blockchain:

Security and Decentralization: Blockchain presents a decentralized approach to digital identity management. Because each person is in charge of their identity data, there is less chance of centralized data breaches.

Immutable Records: Data about a person's identity kept on a blockchain cannot be altered. Once recorded, information is added to an immutable ledger, which improves the data's dependability and integrity.

Self-Sovereign Identity (SSI): The idea of self-sovereign identity, in which people are in complete control of their own attributes, is supported by blockchain technology. This improves privacy by giving users the ability to provide information only when necessary.

3. Important Elements of Blockchain-Based Digital Identity:

Decentralized Identifiers (DIDs): DIDs are distinct blockchain-based identifiers linked to certain individuals. They are the cornerstone upon which self-governing digital identities are built.

Verifiable credentials are digital attestations or proofs that validate particular parts of an individual's identification and are provided by reliable organizations like governments or financial institutions. Credentials that can be verified are safely kept on the blockchain.

4. Blockchain Applications for Digital Identity:

Access Management: By giving consumers more choice over who can access their personal data, blockchain-based digital identities lessen the need for centralized authentication solutions.

Cross-Border Identity Verification: People can access services and establish their identities in several jurisdictions thanks to blockchain's safe and effective cross-border identity verification.

Credentialing and Qualifications: Verifiable credentials can be issued on the blockchain by educational institutions, employers, and certification authorities, guaranteeing the legitimacy of qualifications.

5. Privacy-Related Issues:

Zero-Knowledge Proofs: Zero-knowledge proofs are a common feature of blockchain solutions that let people validate information without disclosing the original data. This preserves privacy while still allowing for the required verification.

6. Problems and Upcoming Changes:

Interoperability: It's still difficult to make various blockchain-based identity solutions work together. To solve this issue, continuous standardization initiatives are underway.

Regulatory Compliance: As digital identity systems advance, there will be obstacles to overcome, including ensuring compliance with data protection regulations and adjusting to current regulatory frameworks.

The blockchain-based digital identity signifies a paradigm shift in the way people handle and govern their personal data. We may anticipate that digital identification solutions will be crucial in changing the identity verification and authentication landscape as standardization initiatives and technical breakthroughs move forward.

d. Industries That Could Gain from Blockchain: Increasing Innovation and Productivity in All Sectors

Blockchain technology has the power to completely transform a number of industries by bringing efficiency, transparency, and new approaches to enduring problems. These ideas are based on decentralization, transparency, and security. Let's examine the potential advantages of blockchain adoption for various businesses.

1. Banking and related services:

Cross-Border Payments: By doing away with middlemen, cutting expenses, and enabling almost instantaneous settlement, blockchain technology streamlines and expedites cross-border transactions.

Banking with Smart Contracts: By automating procedures like loan approvals, settlements, and regulatory compliance, smart contracts streamline operations and lower the possibility of mistakes.

2. Medical Care:

Safeguarding Health Data: Blockchain technology guarantees the safe and compatible handling of medical records, giving patients more authority over their information while maintaining confidentiality and accuracy.

Drug Traceability: Blockchain technology can be used to track pharmaceuticals throughout their whole supply chain, increasing transparency and lowering the possibility of fake medications.

3. Management of the Supply Chain:

Provenance & Authenticity: Blockchain ensures product authenticity, lowers counterfeiting, and builds consumer trust by offering a visible and verifiable record of the whole supply chain.

Effective logistical: By automating logistical procedures, smart contracts improve supply chain efficiency overall, minimize delays, and optimize inventory management.

4. Property:

Blockchain makes real estate transactions easier and more automated by facilitating the use of smart contracts for escrow services, property transfers, and the automatic fulfillment of contract terms.

Transparent Property Ownership data: Blockchain reduces fraud and conflicts by ensuring transparency and security in property ownership data.

5. Learning:

Verification of Credentials: Blockchain makes it easier to issue credentials that can be verified, including degrees and certificates, guaranteeing their legitimacy and eliminating the need for drawn-out verification procedures.

Transparent Accreditation: By using blockchain technology, educational institutions may keep tamper-proof, transparent accreditation records that serve as a trustworthy resource for evaluating student qualifications.

6. Power:

Decentralized Energy Trading: By allowing the development of decentralized energy systems where anyone may directly purchase and sell excess energy, blockchain technology helps to lessen dependency on centralized utilities.

Carbon Credit Tracking: By enabling transparency in environmental projects and bolstering sustainability efforts, blockchain can be used to track and verify carbon credits.

7. Governance and Law:

Legal agreements can be automated and enforced with the help of smart contracts, which eliminates the need for middlemen and guarantees a transparent and safe execution process.

Secure Voting Systems: By improving voting systems' security and transparency, blockchain helps to reduce fraud risk and guarantee election integrity.

8. Shop:

Customer Loyalty Programs: By facilitating easy award tracking and guaranteeing transparency in program operations, blockchain technology can safeguard and optimize customer loyalty programs.

Supply Chain Visibility: Retailers can track and confirm the authenticity of products by using blockchain technology to improve supply chain visibility.

9. Communications:

Secure Identity Verification: By lowering fraud risk and enhancing user data security, blockchain improves identity verification in telecoms.

Billing and Settlement: By streamlining these procedures across telecom providers, blockchain can minimize disagreements and improve the efficiency of financial transactions.

Blockchain's influence on a wide range of businesses is expected to increase as technology develops further. The potential for beneficial transformations and the encouraging of creativity across sectors can be attributed to the decentralized and transparent character of blockchain technology.

Opportunities for Earnings

a. Long-Term Bitcoin Investments: Getting to Know the Way to Financial Development

Those looking to accumulate wealth over the long run now consider investing in Bitcoin as a major option. Despite its somewhat erratic price, a lot of investors see Bitcoin as a hedge against conventional financial risks and a store of value. For individuals wishing to take advantage of Bitcoin's potential, it is imperative to comprehend the subtleties of long-term investment.

1. Bitcoin as Electronic Gold

Store of Value: In the digital world, Bitcoin is frequently compared to gold and is prized for its rarity as well as the hope that its value will hold and increase over time.

Restricted Supply: Bitcoin's 21 million coin supply is capped, simulating the scarcity of precious metals and generating a deflationary asset.

2. Historical Achievement:

Price Appreciation: Over time, Bitcoin has experienced significant price growth, with notable bull markets providing early investors with large profits.

Market Cycles: The price of bitcoin typically moves in cycles, going through spikes in value followed by dips. Making educated selections as an investor can be aided by knowledge of these cycles.

3. Advantages of Diversification

Portfolio Diversification: Since the performance of Bitcoin may not be correlated with that of conventional assets like equities and bonds, its inclusion in a varied investment portfolio may help to lower overall risk.

Uncorrelated Asset: Investors wishing to increase the diversification of their portfolios may find Bitcoin to be an appealing alternative due to its lack of correlation with conventional financial markets.

4. Dangers and Things to Think About:

Volatility: The price of bitcoin has the ability to fluctuate significantly over short periods of time. Investors need to be patient and ready for market fluctuations.

Regulatory Landscape: The laws that govern Bitcoin are always changing, and these changes may have an effect on how widely accepted and accessible bitcoin is.

5. Long-Term Strategies for Holding:

HODLing: The acronym "HODL" was coined to describe a strategy employed by long-term Bitcoin holders. It was first used to refer to a misspelled word in a forum post. HODLers favor holding onto their Bitcoin during short-term trade swings as opposed to short-term trading.

Dollar-Cost Averaging (DCA): In DCA, a certain amount is consistently invested in Bitcoin, regardless of the cryptocurrency's price. The goal of this approach is to lessen the effect of market volatility on the performance of investments as a whole.

6. Safekeeping and Protection:

Secure Wallets: To guard against potential hackers or illegal access, long-term investors should place a high priority on keeping their Bitcoin in secure wallets, such as hardware wallets or paper wallets.

Private Keys: The security of long-term Bitcoin holdings depends on your comprehension of their significance and your ability to keep secure control over them.

7. Continued Investigation and Observation:

industry Trends: To make well-informed decisions, it is imperative to continuously track technology advancements, regulatory changes, and industry trends.

Educational Resources: Making wise investing decisions requires being up to date on the principles of Bitcoin, blockchain technology, and the larger cryptocurrency scene.

Even while investing in Bitcoin over the long term has the potential to increase wealth, it's critical that investors approach the game knowing exactly what dangers there are, how the market works, and why a disciplined approach is necessary. Investors can use Bitcoin to walk the path to long-term wealth accumulation by taking a deliberate and informed approach.

b. Making Money by Taking Part in Blockchain Projects: Managing the Decentralized Environment

As the blockchain ecosystem is decentralized and inventive, participating in blockchain initiatives offers a wide variety of revenue potential. People can take advantage of a variety of opportunities to earn rewards and actively participate in the developing blockchain environment, such as staking, governance, and contributing to decentralized apps (DApps).

1. Proof of Stake (PoS) and Staking:

Rewarding Members: A lot of blockchain networks use the Proof of Stake (PoS) consensus method, which enables members to use the cryptocurrency holdings they own as security. They receive incentives in exchange for their assistance in network security and transaction validation.

Long-Term Commitment: Staking frequently necessitates the locking up of cash for a predetermined amount of time, which encourages long-term network commitment.

2. Participation in Governance:

Decentralized Autonomous Organizations (DAOs): DAOs give users a voice in how a blockchain project is decided upon. Owners of governance tokens have the ability to vote on proposals and change the course of the project.

prizes for Active Governance: Offering prizes to participants encourages a sense of community service and interest alignment.

3. Produce Farming and Supplying Liquidity:

Supplying Liquidity: Yield farming is supplying liquidity to pools or decentralized exchanges, usually in return for extra tokens or a portion of transaction fees.

Risk considerations: generate farming carries some risks, such as the potential for temporary loss and smart contract vulnerabilities, even if it can generate lucrative profits.

4. Making a contribution to DApps (decentralized applications):

Blockchain systems frequently give developers rewards for their contributions to the creation of decentralized applications. This could entail developing interfaces, constructing smart contracts, or improving the features of already-existing DApps.

Community Engagement: Contributing to open-source projects, interacting with the community, and offering comments can all result in incentives and recognition.

5. Non-Fungible Tokens, or NFTs:

Making and Selling NFTs: With the popularity of NFTs, musicians, artists, and content producers now have the chance to tokenize their creations and sell them straight to collectors.

Taking Part in NFT Marketplaces: By trading, compiling collections, or managing decentralized NFT applications, individuals can also profit from taking part in NFT marketplaces.

6. Consulting and Freelance Work:

Blockchain Consultancy: People with knowledge of smart contract creation, blockchain technology, or security auditing can provide blockchain projects with independent contractors or consultants.

Content Creators: By creating tutorials, instructional materials, or analyses about blockchain projects and technologies, content creators can make money.

7. Operating Validators and Nodes:

Network Security: On some blockchain networks, the operation of nodes or validators adds to the network's security and decentralization. Participants may receive incentives in the form of cryptocurrencies in exchange.

Technical Requirements: Technical expertise and adherence to network specifications are necessary for the setup and upkeep of nodes.

8. Giveaways of tokens and airdrops:

Free Token Distribution: In order to raise capital for their ecosystem, some blockchain projects give away free tokens, or "airdrops," to current holders or community members.

Requirements for Participation: In order to be eligible for airdrops, participants may need to fulfill certain requirements, such as possessing a minimum amount of a specific cryptocurrency.

New revenue streams could appear as the blockchain industry develops, giving people innovative methods to interact with decentralized networks. Participants must make sure they have done their homework, are aware of the risks involved in each opportunity, and match their involvement with their risk tolerance and goals.

C. Careers in the Cryptocurrency Sector: Managing the Changing Work Environment

The cryptocurrency market has grown to be a multifaceted ecosystem with a wide range of job opportunities. For those looking to work in the digital financial space, the industry offers a dynamic work landscape, ranging from non-technical roles in marketing and compliance to technical roles in blockchain development.

1. Blockchain Engineering and Development:

Blockchain developers are in charge of developing and managing smart contracts, decentralized apps (DApps), and blockchain protocols.

Developers of Smart Contracts: Experts in creating and executing smart contracts on blockchain networks that automate and carry out predetermined conditions.

2. Analysis and Trading of Cryptocurrencies:

Cryptocurrency traders: Purchase and sell cryptocurrencies on different exchanges, using research and market trends to guide their trades.

Technical and fundamental analysis is carried out by market analysts to offer insights into market trends, price movements, and possible investment opportunities.

3. Safety and Adherence:

Experts in blockchain security should concentrate on making sure blockchain networks are secure, spotting security holes, and putting countermeasures in place to fend off online attacks.

Compliance Officers: Monitor compliance with regulations and legal frameworks across jurisdictions for cryptocurrency enterprises.

4. Community management and marketing:

Community managers oversee social media accounts, forums, and online communities in order to promote interaction and communication within the cryptocurrency community.

Content marketers should produce and disseminate content to raise awareness of cryptocurrency brands, educate the public, and support blockchain initiatives.

5. Journalism on cryptocurrency and content creation:

Journalists covering the cryptocurrency space: Write about stories, advancements, and patterns while offering the public commentary and insights.

Podcasters and YouTubers: Produce multi-media content that discusses different facets of blockchain technology, cryptocurrencies, and market trends.

6. Customer Relations and Support:

Customer support for cryptocurrencies: Offer prompt, efficient assistance to users in resolving problems with wallets, exchanges, and other services.

Relationship managers: Establish and preserve connections with customers, partners, and other stakeholders in the cryptocurrency industry.

7. Investigation and Creation:

Blockchain Researchers: Investigate and develop blockchain technology through research, helping to create new solutions and protocols.

Economists that specialize in cryptocurrencies should examine the financial aspects of the space, such as market trends, adoption trends, and the effects of regulatory changes.

8. Instruction and Practice:

Blockchain Teachers: Conduct workshops and online courses to teach people about smart contract development, cryptocurrency trading, and blockchain technology.

Technical Trainers: Provide professionals and developers wishing to advance their knowledge in blockchain-related domains with training courses.

9. Project Administration:

Blockchain Project Managers: Keep an eye on the creation and execution of blockchain projects, making sure they adhere to quality standards, budgetary restrictions, and timetables.

10. Startups and Entrepreneurship:

Cryptocurrency entrepreneurs: Found and run cryptocurrency firms, bringing new ideas to the table in areas like blockchain technology, non-fungible tokens (NFTs), and decentralized finance (DeFi).

11. Roles in Law and Regulation:

Blockchain attorneys: Focus on the legal facets of the cryptocurrency sector, offering advice on matters pertaining to contracts, intellectual property, and regulatory compliance.

The explosive growth of the cryptocurrency industry provides a wide range of career options for people with different skill sets. For individuals who are enthusiastic about making a difference in the dynamic field of digital finance, there are plenty of career opportunities in technical development, marketing, compliance, and entrepreneurship. Those who are interested in working in the cryptocurrency sector should keep up with current developments in the field, develop their skills consistently, and look into career paths that fit their interests and areas of competence.

Investments in Cryptocurrencies

a. An Overview of Cryptocurrency Investing: Managing the Digital Financial Opportunities Frontier

Investments in cryptocurrencies have become a prominent and revolutionary feature of the financial scene, providing people with hitherto unheard-of chances to engage in the decentralized realm of digital assets. Comprehending the fundamentals of cryptocurrency investments is imperative for individuals seeking to investigate this swiftly changing and inventive industry.

1. Specifying Investments in Cryptocurrencies:

Digital Assets: Virtual or digital assets that use cryptography for security are known as cryptocurrencies. They function on decentralized networks, frequently built on top of blockchain technology, which guarantees transaction immutability and transparency.

Investment Vehicles: Investments in cryptocurrencies include a range of assets, such as tokens linked to particular projects and alternative coins (altcoins), which are in addition to well-known cryptocurrencies like Ethereum and Bitcoin.

2. Motivations for Investing in Cryptocurrencies:

Decentralization: By operating on decentralized networks, cryptocurrencies provide a degree of financial autonomy and lessen dependency on established financial institutions.

Possibility for Large Returns: Due to the market's notorious volatility, there may be chances for investors to receive sizable returns.

Diversification: Investing in cryptocurrencies gives investors access to a distinct asset class that expands their portfolios beyond conventional stocks, bonds, and real estate.

Technological Potential and Innovation: The inventiveness of blockchain technology and its potential for game-changing applications in a range of sectors attract investors.

3. Types of Investments in Cryptocurrencies:

Bitcoin (BTC): The original and most well-known cryptocurrency, Bitcoin is sometimes referred to as "digital gold." It is frequently regarded by investors as a hedge against inflation and a store of value.

Altcoins: Beyond Bitcoin, a wide variety of digital assets are represented by alternative cryptocurrencies, or altcoins. Litecoin, Ethereum, Ripple, and other cryptocurrencies have special features and applications.

Token Offerings: Investors can support new projects by buying tokens through Initial Coin Offerings (ICOs) and Security Token Offerings (STOs). Risks and regulatory issues, however, must be carefully considered.

4. Investment Methodologies:

Long-Term Holding (HODLing): The practice of holding onto cryptocurrency for a considerable amount of time, frequently with the hope that its value will increase over time.

Day trading is the short-term buying and selling of cryptocurrencies with the goal of profiting from changes in price in a single day.

Dollar-Cost Averaging (DCA): Investing a fixed amount in cryptocurrencies at regular intervals, regardless of market conditions, to reduce the impact of volatility.

5. Risk Considerations:

Volatility: Cryptocurrency markets are known for their price volatility, which can result in significant fluctuations within short time frames.

Regulatory Risks: Evolving regulatory environments can impact the accessibility and acceptance of cryptocurrencies in different jurisdictions.

Security Concerns: Cryptocurrency investments require secure storage and protection of private keys to guard against theft and hacking.

6. Research and Due Diligence:

Project Evaluation: Thoroughly researching and evaluating the fundamentals of a cryptocurrency project, including its technology, team, use case, and community support.

Market Analysis: Staying informed about market trends, news, and potential catalysts that can impact the value of cryptocurrencies.

7. Wallets and Exchanges:

Secure Storage: Choosing secure wallets, such as hardware wallets or reputable software wallets, for storing cryptocurrencies.

Reputable Exchanges: Selecting reputable cryptocurrency exchanges with strong security measures, user-friendly interfaces, and a diverse range of supported assets.

8. Portfolio Management:

Diversification: Balancing a cryptocurrency portfolio by investing in a variety of assets to spread risk.

Regular Review: Periodically reassessing the portfolio, adjusting holdings based on market conditions, and rebalancing to align with investment goals.

As individuals navigate the world of cryptocurrency investments, education, research, and a strategic approach are essential. Whether driven by the desire for financial autonomy, diversification, or participation in innovative technologies, investors should approach the digital frontier with a clear understanding of the risks, opportunities, and the evolving nature of the cryptocurrency market.

b. Portfolio Diversification in Cryptocurrency Investments: Balancing Risk and Reward

Diversifying a cryptocurrency portfolio is a fundamental strategy aimed at managing risk and optimizing potential returns. While the digital asset market offers numerous investment opportunities, the principle of spreading investments across different assets remains key to building a resilient and well-balanced portfolio.

1. The Rationale for Portfolio Diversification:

Risk Mitigation: Cryptocurrency markets are known for their volatility, and individual assets can experience significant price fluctuations. Diversification helps mitigate the impact of adverse movements in any single asset on the overall portfolio.

Capturing Opportunities: Different cryptocurrencies may have unique value propositions, use cases, and growth potential. Diversification allows investors to participate in a broader spectrum of opportunities within the market.

2. Types of Cryptocurrencies for Diversification:

Major Cryptocurrencies: Core cryptocurrencies like Bitcoin (BTC) and Ethereum (ETH) often serve as foundational elements in diversified portfolios, providing stability and liquidity.

Mid and Small-Cap Altcoins: Investing in a range of mid and small-cap altcoins introduces additional growth opportunities. These projects may have higher risk but can also offer substantial returns.

Stablecoins: Stablecoins, pegged to fiat currencies like the US Dollar, provide a hedge against market volatility and serve as a stable store of value during market downturns.

3. Industry and Sector Exposure:

Blockchain Platforms: Investing in the infrastructure of blockchain technology, such as platforms like Ethereum, Binance Smart Chain, or Solana, can provide exposure to the growth of decentralized applications.

DeFi (Decentralized Finance): Including decentralized finance projects in a portfolio allows investors to participate in the disruption of traditional financial services.

NFTs (Non-Fungible Tokens): Exposure to the burgeoning NFT space, with tokens representing unique digital assets, adds a creative and potentially lucrative dimension to a diversified portfolio.

4. Geographic Diversification:

Regional Focus: Considering cryptocurrencies with regional relevance or unique applications can enhance diversification. Different regions may have distinct regulatory environments and market dynamics.

Global Stablecoins: Including stablecoins from different jurisdictions can provide stability while considering the regulatory landscape in various parts of the world.

5. Risk Tolerance and Investment Horizon:

Balancing Risk and Reward: Diversification should align with an investor's risk tolerance and investment goals. While higher-risk assets may offer greater potential returns, they also come with increased volatility.

Long-Term vs. Short-Term Strategies: The investment horizon plays a role in portfolio diversification. Long-term investors may focus on fundamental projects, while short-term traders may diversify to capture short-lived opportunities.

6. Regular Monitoring and Rebalancing:

Market Conditions: The cryptocurrency market is dynamic, and assets may perform differently under changing conditions. Regularly monitoring market trends, news, and project developments is crucial.

Rebalancing Strategies: Periodically reassessing the portfolio's performance and adjusting allocations based on market dynamics, new opportunities, and evolving investment goals.

7. Security and Storage Considerations:

Secure Storage: Each asset in a diversified portfolio requires secure storage. Utilizing reputable hardware wallets, software wallets, or custody services ensures the protection of private keys.

Diligence in Exchanges: Choosing reliable and secure cryptocurrency exchanges for trading and managing the portfolio, considering factors such as security features, liquidity, and reputation.

8. Ongoing Research and Education:

Market Trends: Staying informed about emerging trends, technological advancements, and regulatory developments in the cryptocurrency space enhances the ability to make informed diversification decisions.

Continuous Learning: The cryptocurrency industry evolves swiftly. Engaging in continual learning, attending industry conferences, and being abreast of educational resources contribute to effective portfolio management.

By systematically diversifying a cryptocurrency portfolio, investors can possibly boost resilience, optimize returns, and negotiate the volatility character of the digital asset market. It is vital for people to adjust their diversification strategy to their personal risk tolerance, investing goals, and the shifting environment of the bitcoin sector.

C. Risks and Tips for Beginner Investors in Cryptocurrency: Navigating the New Frontier with Caution

Entering the world of cryptocurrencies as a rookie investor offers great potential, but it also comes with inherent hazards. Understanding these dangers and employing sensible solutions can help secure investments and enable a positive and informed introduction into the dynamic field of digital assets.

1. Risks for Beginner Investors:

Market Volatility: Cryptocurrency marketplaces are known for their price volatility, with prices often witnessing considerable swings over short periods. This might result in both rapid gains and losses.

legal Uncertainty: The legal landscape for cryptocurrencies is developing, and changes in legislation can effect market accessibility, project development, and overall investor confidence.

Security Concerns: The potential of hacking, scams, and fraudulent operations is rampant in the cryptocurrency field. Ensuring secure storage of private keys and using trustworthy exchanges is vital.

Lack of Investor Protection: Cryptocurrency investments are not guaranteed or covered by traditional financial institutions, exposing investors to a higher degree of risk compared to traditional assets.

Market Manipulation: Due to the relatively low market capitalization of some cryptocurrencies, they may be susceptible to price manipulation by larger holders or external parties.

Technological Risks: Technical flaws, software faults, and network issues can impair the functioning and security of blockchain applications.

2. Tips for Beginner Investors:

Educate Yourself: Before investing, take the time to learn the foundations of blockchain technology, other cryptocurrencies, and the general market dynamics. Knowledge is a great weapon in negotiating the complexity of the crypto realm.

Start Small: Begin with a tiny investment that you can afford to lose. This strategy allows you to gain experience without exposing yourself to major financial danger.

Diversify Your Portfolio: Spread your money among multiple cryptocurrencies and projects. Diversification helps lessen the impact of poor-performing assets on the entire portfolio.

Conduct Thorough Research: Prioritize projects with strong fundamentals, experienced teams, clear use cases, and community support. Research whitepapers, roadmaps, and project updates before making investment decisions.

Risk Management: Establish explicit risk tolerance thresholds and set stop-loss orders when applicable. Avoid investing more than you can afford to lose, and resist the desire to seek quick riches.

Secure Storage: Use secure wallets, like as hardware wallets, to store your cryptocurrencies. Be cautious when leaving assets on exchanges, as they may be subject to hackers.

Stay Informed: Regularly update yourself on market trends, news, and project developments. Being aware of macroeconomic trends and regulatory developments might help you make informed decisions.

Avoid FOMO (Fear of Missing Out): Emotional decision-making, motivated by FOMO or panic selling, can lead to inferior outcomes. Stay disciplined and stick to your investment approach.

Seek Professional Advice: If needed, engage financial advisors with expertise in cryptocurrency. They can provide individualized advise based on your financial goals and risk tolerance.

Participate in Communities: Joining bitcoin communities, forums, or social media groups allows you to learn from experienced investors, share thoughts, and keep connected with the latest industry conversations.

Navigating the cryptocurrency market as a beginner includes a learning curve, but with careful assessment of risks and application of cautious techniques, investors can position themselves for a good and informed journey into the exciting world of digital assets.

Cryptocurrency Mining

a. What is Mining and How it Works:

Cryptocurrency mining is the process by which new units of a digital currency are produced and transactions are added to the blockchain. It requires solving complicated mathematical problems that validate and safeguard transactions, maintaining the integrity of the decentralized ledger. Here's a closer look at how mining operates:

1. Proof-of-Work (PoW) Mechanism:

Mining Nodes: In a PoW-based cryptocurrency network, miners operate nodes, which are powerful computers connected to the blockchain. These nodes compete to solve cryptographic riddles.

Transaction Validation: Miners bundle together pending transactions into blocks and compete to solve a complex mathematical challenge relating to the block's content. The first miner to solve the riddle announces the solution to the network.

Consensus and Block Addition: Once a solution is verified by other nodes, the new block is added to the blockchain. This method ensures the consensus mechanism and secures the network against fraudulent transactions.

2. Mining Hardware:

ASIC (Application-Specific Integrated Circuit) Miners: As cryptocurrency mining has grown, specialized hardware known as ASIC miners has become widespread for PoW-based cryptocurrencies like Bitcoin. These gadgets are built primarily for efficient and high-speed mining.

GPU (Graphics Processing Unit) Mining: Some cryptocurrencies, like Ethereum, are resistant to ASIC miners, making GPU mining a popular alternative. GPUs are powerful graphics cards that excel at parallel processing activities.

3. Proof-of-Stake (PoS) Mechanism:

Validator Nodes: In PoS-based networks, validators are chosen to create new blocks and validate transactions depending on the amount of cryptocurrency they possess as collateral. The more bitcoin possessed, the higher the possibility of being selected.

Consensus Without Intensive Computing: Unlike PoW, PoS does not require miners to solve complicated mathematical puzzles. Instead, validators are selected to construct new blocks in a deterministic manner.

4. Mining Rewards:

Block Rewards: Miners are rewarded with newly minted cryptocurrency coins for successfully adding a new block to the network. This mechanism introduces fresh coins into circulation and incentivizes miners to contribute computational power.

Transaction Fees: In addition to block rewards, miners may get transaction fees paid by customers for speedier transaction processing.

5. Network Security and Decentralization:

Resisting Attacks: Mining strengthens the security of the bitcoin network by making it computationally expensive for bad actors to modify the blockchain. The decentralized nature of mining contributes to the resilience of the network against attackers.

Ensuring Consensus: Miners, by their computational efforts, ensure that a consensus is formed on the state of the blockchain. This consensus is crucial for the trustworthiness and immutability of the distributed ledger.

6. Environmental Considerations:

Energy Consumption: PoW mining, particularly in large-scale operations, can require enormous quantities of energy.

Discussions concerning the effects of bitcoin mining on the environment have resulted from this.

Transition to Sustainable Solutions: In an effort to save energy and advance sustainability, certain cryptocurrencies are investigating or putting into practice alternative consensus techniques like Proof-of-Stake or hybrid models.

Gaining knowledge about the complexities of bitcoin mining can help one better understand blockchain networks' foundation. Miners support the security, decentralization, and usefulness of the digital currencies they support, whether by contributing processing power through PoW or using collateral-based consensus through PoS.

b. Diversifying Your Portfolio: Juggling Mining Projects for the Best Returns

One way to generate digital assets is through cryptocurrency mining, which adds a special dimension to portfolio diversification. Mining introduces an element of active engagement to traditional investments, which mostly include acquiring and holding various cryptocurrencies. To achieve the best results, miners can diversify their holdings in the following ways:

1. Multiple Cryptocurrency Mining:

Multicurrency Mining: By spreading out mining activities over several cryptocurrencies, one can reduce the risk brought on by an asset's price fluctuation. In order to mine more than one coin at once, miners might distribute computational power.

Research and Selection: The efficiency of multicurrency mining is increased when cryptocurrencies are selected based on in-depth analysis of their fundamentals, growth potential, and compatibility with individual investment objectives.

2. Partial-Stake (PoS) and Proof-of-Work (PoW) Mining Equilibrium

Hybrid Mining Techniques: By combining PoW and PoS mining, some miners decide to diversify their holdings. This enables them to make use of various consensus-building techniques, resulting in a more varied and well-rounded strategy.

Risk Reduction: PoS mining provides a more energy-efficient option compared to PoW mining, which is recognized for being energy-intensive. Maintaining active participation in the mining ecosystem while reducing environmental concerns is made possible by striking a balance between the two approaches.

3. Assessment of Mining Pools:

Diverse Mining Pools: In order to improve their chances of solving blocks and winning rewards, miners frequently join mining pools, which pool their total computing power. The risk posed by a single pool's performance or outage is reduced by diversifying over several mining pools.

Payout Structures: In order to effectively diversify a portfolio in the mining industry, it is necessary to comprehend the fees, reputation, and payout structures of mining pools.

4. Algorithms for mining and hardware:

Adapting to Algorithm Changes: In order to increase security or efficiency, cryptocurrency projects may decide to adjust their consensus algorithms. Maintaining involvement and profitability requires diversifying mining hardware to adjust to modifications in mining algorithms.

Flexibility in gear Selection: Specific gear may be needed for mining several coins. To meet the specific needs of different mining operations, miners might expand the variety of hardware in their portfolio.

5. Profitability and Risk Management:

Comprehending Market Dynamics: Variations in coin prices, network complexity, or reward structures can all affect how profitable mining is in cryptocurrency markets. Diversification facilitates risk distribution and allows for market circumstance adaptation.

Monitoring Performance: Miners can reallocate resources based on current market trends and the possibility of optimal returns by routinely evaluating the performance of various mining endeavors.

6. Regulatory and Environmental Considerations:

Handling Regulatory Changes: The viability and profitability of cryptocurrency mining operations may be impacted by regulatory changes. Diversification among different geographic areas helps lessen the effects of regulatory uncertainty.

Measures for Sustainability: Miners may decide to diversify their operations by introducing more energy-efficient technology or by investigating sustainable mining techniques in response to environmental concerns.

When mining cryptocurrencies, portfolio diversification is a tactical move that helps miners negotiate the always changing and dynamic world of digital assets. Through prudent allocation of resources among various cryptocurrencies, mining pools, hardware choices, and consensus processes, miners can optimize the robustness and financial viability of their mining ventures.

C. Dangers and Advice for Novice Investors: Proceed Cautiously on the Mining Frontier

Starting to mine cryptocurrencies as a novice presents both thrilling possibilities and possible dangers. A successful and well-informed introduction into the mining industry requires an understanding of these dangers and the implementation of effective methods. Here is a thorough rundown of the dangers and advice for inexperienced miners:

1. Hazards for Novice Miners:

Initial Investment: Purchasing mining hardware may necessitate a substantial outlay of funds. Before beginning mining operations, novices should thoroughly evaluate their financial situation and budget.

Technological Complexity: It can be difficult to set up and configure mining hardware, software, and mining pools. Inadequate comprehension or inexperience could result in operational problems or inefficiency.

Market Volatility: Changes in the market might affect the value of cryptocurrencies that are mined. Beginners need to be aware that the volatility of the cryptocurrency market can have an impact on the profits they receive from mining.

Energy Costs: Mining activities can use a lot of electricity, especially Proof-of-Work (PoW) mining. Novices should investigate energy-efficient mining solutions and think about how it will affect their energy expenses.

Network complexity: The complexity of resolving mining puzzles rises as more miners join the network. This may have an effect on how frequently blocks are successfully mined and, as a result, how profitable mining operations are overall.

2. Advice for Novice Miners:

Educate Yourself: Give top priority to learning everything there is to know about mining principles, such as how to choose hardware, how to use mining algorithms, and how mining software operates.

Start Small: To get a feel for the procedure and reduce the dangers associated with your first investment, think about starting with a basic mining setup. Scaling up can be a slow process that happens as confidence and knowledge increase.

Selecting the Correct Hardware: Examine and choose mining hardware according to features including hash rate, energy efficiency, and algorithm compatibility. Think about mining alternatives with both ASIC and GPU depending on the cryptocurrency you are targeting.

Join Reputable Mining Pools: By joining mining pools, you can increase your chances of winning rewards on a regular basis.

Select trustworthy pools that have a track record of consistent payouts and clear pricing schedules.

Regularly Monitor Operations: Pay close attention to how well the mining equipment is operating as well as the operation as a whole. Check for updates often, take care of technical problems right away, and make efficient use of the settings.

Diversify Your Mining Ventures: Take into Account Spreading Your Mining Operations Among Various Cryptocurrencies, Mining Pools, and Algorithms. This strategy improves flexibility in response to changes in the market and helps disperse risk.

Comprehend Network Difficulty: Be aware that mining profitability may be impacted by network difficulty. Keep an eye out for variations in the degree of difficulty and modify your mining tactics accordingly.

Control Energy Costs: Look at mining options that use less energy and evaluate how this will affect your electricity costs. To maximize operating costs, take into account variables including location, energy rates, and hardware efficiency.

Keep Up with Market Trends: Remain current with technology innovations, regulatory changes in the cryptocurrency realm, and market trends. Making better decisions is aided by knowledge of the larger industry dynamics.

Starting out in the mining industry demands a combination of knowledge, foresight, and flexibility. Beginners can increase their chances of having a profitable and satisfying mining experience by adopting responsible risk management techniques and approaching cryptocurrency mining with an informed mentality.

Mining Cryptocurrencies

a. Definition of mining and its process:

The foundation of decentralized digital currencies is cryptocurrency mining, which offers a way to verify transactions, protect networks, and create new coins. Fundamentally, mining is the use of computing techniques to solve challenging mathematical riddles. This is an in-depth examination of what mining is and how it functions:

1. Mechanism for Proof-of-Work (PoW):

Mining Nodes: Miners run nodes, which are strong computers linked to the blockchain in a proof-of-work (PoW) cryptocurrency network. These nodes compete to find answers to riddles in cryptography.

Transaction validation involves miners competing to find the solution to a challenging mathematical puzzle pertaining to the content of blocks made up of pending transactions. The solution is broadcast to the network by the first miner to solve the challenge.

Consensus and Block Addition: A new block is appended to the blockchain after a solution has been validated by additional nodes. This procedure protects the network against fraudulent transactions and guarantees the consensus mechanism.

2. Hardware for mining:

ASIC (Application-Specific Integrated Circuit) Miners: As the world of cryptocurrency mining has developed, dedicated hardware for PoW-based cryptocurrencies, such as Bitcoin, has become commonplace. These gadgets are made especially for quick and effective mining.

GPU (Graphics Processing Unit) mining is a well-liked substitute for ASIC mining for certain cryptocurrencies, such as Ethereum. GPUs are strong graphics cards that perform well on jobs requiring parallel processing.

3. Mechanism for Proof-of-Stake (PoS):

Validator Nodes: Depending on how much cryptocurrency they have pledged as collateral, validators are selected to build fresh blocks and approve transactions in PoS-based networks. The likelihood of being chosen increases with the amount of cryptocurrency possessed.

Consensus Without Intensive Computing: In contrast to PoW, PoS does not need miners to work out challenging arithmetic problems. Rather, deterministically, validators are chosen to generate new blocks.

4. Mining Benefits:

Block Rewards: When miners successfully add a new block to the blockchain, they are rewarded with freshly created bitcoin coins. By doing this, fresh currencies are pushed into circulation and miners are encouraged to provide processing power.

Transaction Fees: Users may pay transaction fees to miners in addition to block rewards in exchange for quicker transaction processing.

5. Decentralization and Network Security:

Defying Attacks: Mining increases the network's security by making it more computationally costly for nefarious actors to alter the blockchain. The decentralized aspect of mining adds to the network's ability to withstand attacks.

Achieving Consensus: Miners use their computational prowess to make sure that there is agreement on the current state of the blockchain. The distributed ledger's dependability and immutability depend on this consensus.

6. Environmental Factors to Be Considered

Energy Consumption: PoW mining can use a lot of energy, especially in large-scale operations. Discussions concerning the effects of bitcoin mining on the environment have resulted from this.

Transition to Sustainable Solutions: In an effort to save energy and advance sustainability, certain cryptocurrencies are investigating or putting into practice alternative consensus techniques like Proof-of-Stake or hybrid models.

Gaining knowledge about the complexities of bitcoin mining can help one better understand blockchain networks' foundation. Miners support the security, decentralization, and usefulness of the digital currencies they support, whether by contributing processing power through PoW or using collateral-based consensus through PoS.

b. Hardware and Software Requirements: Building the Mining Arsenal

Starting a cryptocurrency mining operation involves a hardware and software collection that is specifically designed to meet the requirements of the selected cryptocurrency and consensus method. An in-depth examination of the elements necessary for productive mining operations is provided below:

1. Hardware Parts:

a. ASIC Miners: Specifically designed circuits with a single purpose.

Efficient and Quick: ASIC miners are specialized equipment made just for mining cryptocurrencies. Because of their superior speed and efficiency, they are the go-to option for PoW-based cryptocurrencies like Bitcoin.

Algorithm Specificity: Certain mining algorithms are handled by ASIC miners in their configuration. For instance, the SHA-256 method used by Bitcoin necessitates the use of ASIC miners specifically designed for this cryptographic task.

b. GPU miners, or graphics processing units:

Versatility: GPUs can handle a wide range of mining algorithms, making them more adaptable than ASIC miners. They are frequently used to mine PoW-based coins like Ethereum, which are resistant to ASIC centralization.

Algorithm Adaptability: GPU miners provide flexibility for miners who want to switch between multiple cryptocurrencies since they can adapt to changes in mining algorithms.

c. Mining Equipment Setup and Rigs:

Mining rig configurations: In order to optimize computing power, mining rigs are setups that include many ASIC or GPU mining units. The scale of mining activities determines the rig layouts, which range from small-scale installations for lone miners to large-scale operations in specialized facilities.

Power Supply Units (PSUs): Mining operations require a reliable and efficient power source. High-capacity PSUs with numerous power connectors are frequently used by miners to guarantee the dependable operation of hardware components.

d. Solutions for Storage:

Operating Systems and Mining Software: Mining software that is compatible with the selected hardware makes it easier for the mining rig and the blockchain network to communicate. Operating systems with higher stability and security, such Linux-based distributions, are frequently used.

External Storage: The blockchain data is stored using external storage solutions, which guarantees that mining will continue even after reboots. USB or other interfaces are usually used to connect to this storage.

2. Components of Software:

a. Software for mining:

Mining Clients: The bitcoin network and the mining gear are connected by means of mining software. Well-known mining customers include NiceHash, BFGMiner, and CGMiner. Miners can join mining pools and adjust their hardware settings with the help of these programs.

Graphical User Interfaces (GUIs): Beginners can more easily configure and monitor their mining activities without requiring the knowledge of command-line interfaces thanks to certain mining software's user-friendly GUIs.

b. Wallets:

Digital wallets: To receive and store the coins that are produced, cryptocurrency wallets are necessary. Wallets can be internet, software- or hardware-based. Protecting a wallet using private keys is essential for preserving profits from mining.

Compatibility of Wallet: Verify that the wallet of choice is compatible with the particular coin being mined. Certain coins suggest using particular wallet providers or have special requirements for wallets.

c. Pools for mining:

Joining Mining Pools: By combining the processing power of several miners, mining pools raise the chances of block solving successfully and generating regular payouts. Slush Pool, F2Pool, and Antpool are a few of the well-known mining pools.

Software Compatibility of the Pool: Pick a mining pool that works with the selected mining program and accepts the desired cryptocurrency.

d. Tools for Monitoring and Optimization:

Hardware Monitoring Tools: Miners can keep an eye on the performance, power usage, and temperature of individual hardware components with the help of programs like MSI Afterburner and HWiNFO. This maximizes mining efficiency and prevents overheating.

Network Monitoring: Tools for monitoring the performance of mining operations track hash rates, accepted shares, and possible problems in real time. Miners can optimize their settings for optimal profitability with the help of this data.

Putting together the ideal set of gear and software is essential for a profitable and effective bitcoin mining business. ASIC or GPU miners, mining rig configurations, mining software, and wallet selections are just a few of the tools that miners must carefully customize to fit their preferred cryptocurrencies and the unique requirements of their mining activities.

C. Profitability Issues: Managing the Mining Industry's Economic Environment

Although mining cryptocurrencies offers the possibility of gaining digital assets, the profitability environment is dynamic and subject to several influences. To maximize their financial results, miners must carefully assess and handle these factors. An examination of the main variables affecting the profitability of bitcoin mining is provided below:

1. Mining Challenge:

Dynamic Adjustments: Depending on the network's overall processing capacity, cryptocurrency networks dynamically modify the mining difficulty. The difficulty of mining grows as more miners join, which may have an effect on the number of blocks that are successfully mined and, in turn, the rewards.

Impact on Profitability: As a result of a reduced chance of block solution for individual miners, higher mining difficulty might have an adverse effect on the overall profitability of mining operations. Miners have to prepare for and adjust to variations in network difficulties.

2. Security of the Network and Hash Rate:

Significance of Hash Rate: The hash rate shows how much processing power has been added to the network. While a higher hash rate improves network security, it may also make miners more competitive.

Balancing Act: Miners should strive for a balanced hash rate that maximizes earnings and makes a significant contribution to the network's stability and security.

3. Coin Values:

Market Volatility: Changes in the market might affect the value of coins that are mined. Cryptocurrency prices directly affect the entire profitability of mining operations; therefore, miners should keep a constant eye on them.

Hedging Techniques: In order to lessen the effects of price volatility, several miners employ hedging techniques. To secure earnings, this might entail selling some of the coins that are produced right away.

4. Costs of Energy:

Energy Efficiency: Especially in Proof-of-Work (PoW) mining, energy usage is a major operational expense for miners. To cut costs, miners can evaluate how energy-efficient their technology is and look into sustainable mining methods.

Location Considerations: By lowering operating costs, mining in areas with cheaper electricity prices or by employing renewable energy sources can increase overall profitability.

5. Fees for the Mining Pool:

Pool Fee Structures: Mining pools take a cut of the rewards they receive as payment for their services. Miners' ought to be informed about these costs and select pools with clear, affordable price schedules.

Pool Performance: A miner's total profitability is directly impacted by the dependability and payout consistency of a mining pool.

6. Costs of Hardware and Upkeep:

Initial Investment: The breakeven point for profitability is influenced by the initial cost of mining hardware, such as ASIC or GPU miners. Miners need to account for both the initial outlay and continuing maintenance expenses.

Equipment Lifespan: The efficiency of mining hardware may decline with age, which could have an effect on total profitability. To keep their equipment operating at peak efficiency, miners should budget for upgrades or replacements.

7. The regulatory landscape

Regulatory Compliance: Modifications to the regulatory environment may have an effect on how profitable and viable mining operations are. Miners need to stay up to date on regulatory changes and make sure local regulations are being followed.

8. Upcoming Technological Advancements:

Technological Developments: New technology and software for mining could lead to more effective and affordable solutions. Keeping up with technical breakthroughs is crucial for miners looking to maximize efficiency.

9. Techniques for Risk Management:

Diversification: To distribute risk and adjust to shifting market conditions, mining operations might be dispersed across a variety of cryptocurrencies, algorithms, or mining pools.

Constant Monitoring: Miners can make well-informed judgments and modify methods for long-term profitability by keeping a close eye on hardware performance, market trends, and network circumstances.

A strategic approach that takes into account internal operational efficiency as well as external market dynamics is necessary to navigate the economic environment of cryptocurrency mining. In the fast-paced world of digital asset mining, miners may improve their chances of long-term profitability by remaining informed, putting risk management techniques into practice, and responding to changing circumstances.

Trading in Cryptocurrencies

a. Fundamental Trading Ideas: Establishing the Groundwork for Profitable Trading

Starting a bitcoin trading adventure necessitates having a firm grasp of the fundamental ideas that serve as the foundation for trading methods. This article explores some of the fundamental ideas that newcomers to the dynamic and frequently unpredictable world of bitcoin trading should know:

1. Limit orders as well as market orders:

Market orders: These are directives to purchase or sell cryptocurrencies right away at the going rate in the market. Although execution is guaranteed, market movements may cause the price to differ somewhat from what was anticipated.

With limit orders, cryptocurrency traders can indicate the price at which they wish to purchase or sell a coin. More control over trade execution is offered by these orders, which are only carried out when the market hits the designated price.

2. Ask and Bid Prices:

Bid Price: The highest amount a buyer is prepared to spend on a cryptocurrency is represented by the bid price. It is the cost at which a trader is able to offload their holdings.

Ask Price: The lowest amount a seller will take for a cryptocurrency is known as the ask price. It is the cost at which an investor can purchase securities.

3. Disperse:

The difference between the market's highest bid and lowest ask prices is known as the spread. A more efficient market and increased liquidity are frequently indicated by a narrower spread.

4. Depth of Market:

Order Book: The order book, which shows the cumulative buy and sell orders at different price points, is a representation of the market depth. Traders assess possible price fluctuations and market sentiment using this information.

5. Charts with candles:

Visualization Tool: Price fluctuations over a given time period are represented visually by candlestick charts. For the selected timeframe, each candlestick shows the opening, closing, high, and low prices.

6. Backing and Opposition:

Support Levels: These are price ranges that, historically, cryptocurrencies have found it difficult to drop below. These levels are frequently seen by traders as possible places to make purchases.

Resistance Levels: These are the price ranges that cryptocurrencies have traditionally had difficulty rising above. These levels can be viewed by traders as possible selling points.

7. Trend Evaluation:

Finding Trends: Traders examine price charts to find patterns, such as bullish (upward) or bearish (downward) movements. Making educated decisions regarding entering or quitting positions is aided by having a solid understanding of trends.

8. Averages that Move:

Smoothed Price Trends: To produce an indicator that follows trends, price data is smoothed using moving averages. They support traders in determining the trend's direction and possible turning points.

9. Risk Control:

Setting Stop-Loss Orders: Stop-loss orders are used by traders to restrict possible losses by selling a cryptocurrency automatically if its price drops to a preset level.

Position Sizing: Deciding how big a trader should take a position depending on how much risk they are willing to take. Position sizing aids in controlling one's exposure to possible losses.

10. Basic Examination:

Assessing Project Fundamentals: A fundamental analysis entails determining the underlying variables that could affect a cryptocurrency's value. The project team, technology, use case, collaborations, and market demand are all included in this.

11. Indicators of technical analysis:

Relative Strength Index, or RSI, is a tool used to gauge how quickly and how much prices fluctuate. It assists in recognizing overbought or oversold situations, which may indicate a market reversal.

The relationship between two moving averages is displayed by the trend-following momentum indicator known as MACD (moving average convergence divergence). It is used by traders to spot possible shifts in trends.

Gaining a strong understanding of these fundamental trading ideas is essential for navigating the intricate cryptocurrency markets. These ideas can help traders create well-thought-out strategies, control risks, and make choices that support their trading objectives.

b. Suggested Trading Platforms for Novices: Selecting the Appropriate Entry Point to the Markets

Choosing a dependable and easy-to-use trading platform is essential for novices entering the bitcoin trading arena. The following is a summary of suggested trading platforms that are user-friendly, feature-rich, and provide a smooth trading experience for novices:

1. Coinbase

User-Friendly Interface: Coinbase is well known for having an easy-to-use interface, which makes it a great option for new users. It makes purchasing, selling, and managing a range of cryptocurrencies easier.

Instructional Materials: To assist novices in grasping fundamental trading principles and market dynamics, Coinbase offers instructional materials in the form of articles and tutorials.

Security Measures: The platform places a high priority on security, putting in place tools like two-factor authentication to protect user accounts.

2. Binance:

Extensive Selection of Cryptocurrencies: Binance gives traders access to a wide range of cryptocurrencies, giving novices a variety of possibilities.

Simple Trading Interface: For traders who want to go deeper into technical analysis, Binance offers sophisticated charting tools in an easy-to-use interface.

Low Trading Fees: The site is well-known for having reasonable trading fees, which help new users save money.

3. Kraken:

Strong Security Features: Kraken places a high priority on security, using cutting-edge safeguards including cold storage for the vast majority of user cash.

Instructional Materials: Kraken provides instructional materials to help novices grasp trading tactics, risk management, and market principles.

Support for Fiat Currency: The platform makes it easier for users to register by allowing deposits and withdrawals in fiat currencies.

4. eToro:

Social Trading Features: One of eToro's most notable features is its social trading platform, which enables novice traders to watch and emulate the moves made by more seasoned traders.

User-Friendly Platform: Designed with beginners in mind, the platform's user-friendly interface makes managing portfolios and placing trades simple.

Copy Trading: With eToro, novice investors can automatically mimic the trades of seasoned investors.

5. Gemini:

Regulatory Compliance: Gemini is a U.S.-based platform that offers a safe trading environment and is renowned for its adherence to regulations.

Gemini provides market analytics and training materials to assist novices in navigating the bitcoin space.

Institutional-Grade Security: To safeguard user funds and personal data, the platform uses institutional-grade security procedures.

6. Robin Hood:

Commission-Free Trading: Robinhood's commission-free trading strategy helped it become well-known and affordable for novices.

Simplified Interface: The platform's simplified interface appeals to traders who want a clear-cut method of doing business.

Fractional Shares: Robinhood is accessible to people with minimal funds since it allows users to invest in fractional shares.

7. KuCoin:

Variety in Cryptocurrency Selection: KuCoin gives users access to a large assortment of cryptocurrencies, resulting in a variety of trading possibilities.

User-Friendly Interface: The platform is appropriate for novices due to its easy-to-use interface and navigation.

Competitive costs: KuCoin offers its native token holders competitive trading costs as well as bonuses.

Beginners should think about things like fee structures, accessibility of cryptocurrencies, security features, convenience of use, and educational materials when choosing a trading platform. It's best to begin with a platform that suits personal tastes and work your way up to more complex features as your trading abilities grow.

C. Technical Analysis and Simplified Trading Strategies: Techniques for Novices

Simplifying trading techniques and grasping the fundamentals of technical analysis can help novices in the bitcoin market make well-informed decisions. For people who are unfamiliar with the trading environment, the following basic tactics and essential technical analysis ideas are recommended:

1. Hold On for Dear Life, or HODLing:

Long-Term Investment: HODLing is the practice of holding onto cryptocurrencies for a considerable amount of time, regardless of momentary market swings.

Psychological Resilience: This tactic, which attempts to endure short-term market volatility, is predicated on the conviction that cryptocurrencies have long-term promise.

2. Average Dollar-Cost (DCA):

Regular Investments: Regardless of the price of the cryptocurrency, DCA entails systematically investing a set amount of money at regular intervals.

Market Volatility Mitigation: By accumulating assets throughout time at different price points, investors can lessen the impact of short-term market volatility.

3. Trend After:

Finding Trends: Finding and adhering to the market's dominant trend, whether it be upward (bullish) or downward (bearish), is the process of trend following.

Simple Moving Averages (SMA): To determine the direction of a trend, beginners can utilize simple moving averages. When the current price is higher than the moving average, a bullish trend is suggested, and vice versa.

4. Trading at Resistance and Support:

Traders see resistance levels as possible selling points and support levels as possible purchasing chances. Buy at Support, Sell at Resistance.

Candlestick Patterns: To obtain insight into possible trend reversals, beginners might utilize candlestick patterns at support or resistance levels.

5. Relative Strength Index, or RSI:

Overbought and Oversold Conditions: RSI is a useful tool for determining whether the market is possibly overbought or oversold.

Thresholds: A value below 30 indicates oversold conditions, pointing to a possible upward advance, and a reading above 70 indicates overbought conditions, suggesting a possible reversal.

6. Crossovers of Moving Averages:

Crossover Signals: To generate buy or sell signals, two separate moving averages (such as a short-term and a long-term) are used in a moving average crossover.

Death Cross and Golden Cross: A golden cross indicates a possible bullish trend when it happens when the short-term moving average crosses above the long-term moving average. Conversely, a death cross suggests a possible bearish trend.

7. Trading Breakout:

Finding Breakout Points: In breakout trading, a position is entered when the price breaks through a key level of support or resistance.

Confirmation and Stop-Loss: Using stop-loss orders and verifying a breakout with higher trading volume are two strategies that can assist control risks.

8. Risk Control:

Establishing Stop-Loss and Take-Profit Orders: Stop-loss orders are used to restrict possible losses, and take-profit orders are used to guarantee profits at predefined levels.

Position Sizing: Deciding how big a trader should take a position depending on how much risk they are willing to take.

For those with no prior experience trading cryptocurrencies, these streamlined approaches offer an introduction to the fundamentals of market dynamics. These tactics must be used in conjunction with continuous education, risk control techniques, and a cautious mindset in order to progressively develop confidence and competence in the ever-changing realm of cryptocurrency trading.

Alternative Ways to Make Money with Cryptocurrencies

a. Using Your Assets to Create Passive Income through Staking

Staking has become a well-liked way for cryptocurrency owners to actively contribute to the security and validity of blockchain networks while earning passive money. To sustain the network's functioning, users must lock up a portion of their money through this method. This is a thorough explanation of staking and how it provides a way to make money with cryptocurrencies:

1. Staking definition:

Taking Part in Network Consensus: In order to take part in the consensus process of a Proof-of-Stake (PoS) or Delegated Proof-of-Stake (DPoS) blockchain network, staking participants, often referred to as validators, entails locking up a certain quantity of their cryptocurrency as collateral.

Securing the Network: Validators are essential to the creation of new blocks, the validation of transactions, and the decentralization and security of the network.

2. The Process of Staking:

Locking Up Cryptocurrency: Staking participants pledge a portion of their holdings to a network wallet or staking contract. The term "stake" is frequently used to describe this locked sum.

Earning Rewards: Based on the quantity of cryptocurrency they have staked; validators are chosen to build new blocks and approve transactions. Validators receive staking benefits in exchange for their work, which are usually in the form of more cryptocurrency.

3. Different Staking Types:

Individual Staking: Users can use a staking platform offered by the blockchain network or operate their own staking node to stake their own cryptocurrency.

Delegated Staking: In Distributed Proof of Stake (DPoS) networks, users can engage in staking without actively managing a node by assigning their stake to a selected validator. A portion of the staking rewards are given to the delegators.

4. Advantages of Partaking in Securities:

Passive Income: By rewarding participants for their contributions to the network's security and consensus, staking provides a passive income stream.

Network Participation: Through staking, cryptocurrency owners can take an active part in the blockchain network's governance and decision-making procedures.

Long-Term Investment: Stakers' motivations are in line with the general well-being of the ecosystem since they frequently have a stake in the network's expansion and success.

5. Dangers and Things to Think About:

Volatility: The total value of staking rewards may be impacted by market volatility in the value of the staked coin.

Slashing: As a punishment for malevolent activity or breaking network rules, validators on certain blockchain networks may lose some of the assets they have staked.

Lock-Up Times: Staked assets frequently have lock-up times that prevent easy access to or withdrawal of the assets.

6. Frequently Used Staking Coins:

Ethereum 2.0 (ETH): With Ethereum 2.0, the network is moving toward a proof-of-work consensus mechanism, enabling users to stake their ETH in order to support it.

Tezos (XTZ): Tezos is a proof-of-work blockchain that allows users to stake their XTZ in order to gain incentives for staking and to take part in consensus.

Cardano (ADA): Cardano is a proof-of-stake (PoS) platform that enables users to stake ADA in order to bolster network security and receive incentives for staking.

Staking offers bitcoin owners a compelling chance to participate in the security and decentralization of blockchain networks while generating passive income. Staking is anticipated to have a major impact on how decentralized finance and blockchain governance develop in the future as the cryptocurrency ecosystem continues to change.

b. Airdrops and Forks: Examining Unexpected Benefits and the Development of Blockchain

Through airdrops and forks, participants in the ever-changing cryptocurrency landscape might profit from unforeseen windfalls. Without actively participating in conventional mining or staking, users can earn extra cryptocurrency assets through both of these novel methods. Now let's explore the ideas behind airdrops and forks and see how they might be profitable in the cryptocurrency market:

1. Airdrops:

Definition: Airdrops are the process of giving away free cryptocurrency tokens or coins to owners of native assets on a particular blockchain. These distributions are frequently started by initiatives aiming to reward current users, create awareness, or establish a new community through bootstrapping.

Participation Requirements: To be eligible for an airdrop, a user must meet certain requirements, such as holding a certain quantity of a particular cryptocurrency, or they must actively use the platform.

Types of Airdrops: There are several varieties of airdrops, such as hard fork, surprise, and bounty drops.

2. How Airdrops Operate

Snapshot Mechanism: The blockchain captures a snapshot of users' balances at a particular block height in order to facilitate airdrops. The airdrop is available to those who had the designated cryptocurrency at the time of the snapshot.

Distribution Procedure: Following the snapshot, eligible addresses receive the new tokens, which are typically distributed in proportion to the amount of held native cryptocurrency. Generally, users must adhere to the project's instructions in order to claim their airdropped tokens.

3. Knives:

Definition: A fork happens when a blockchain experiences a major alteration that creates two new, independent blockchains. Forks come in two primary varieties: soft and hard.

Hard Forks: A hard fork occurs when the blockchain divides into two distinct chains, each following its own set of rules and regulations. Owners of the original cryptocurrency may get an equivalent quantity of the newly forked cryptocurrency, and each chain remains independent.

Soft Forks: Soft forks are blockchain updates that are backwards compatible. Although they usually don't lead to the creation of a new cryptocurrency, they might alter the consensus rules within the network.

4. Opportunities for Earnings:

Distribution of Assets: As holders of the original cryptocurrency may receive additional assets in the form of airdropped tokens or forked coins, airdrops and forks can result in unforeseen riches.

Impact on Market Value: Recipients' total cryptocurrency holdings may see a rise in value, contingent on the acceptance and performance of the new assets.

5. Dangers and Things to Think About:

Scam Airdrops: In order to protect themselves from phishing and scams, participants should be cautious and confirm the authenticity of airdrop announcements.

Value of Forked Coins: Before interacting with or selling recently acquired assets, recipients should carefully weigh the potential risks and rewards as the value of forked coins can fluctuate.

6. Prominent Illustrations:

Bitcoin Cash (BCH): A prominent illustration of a hard fork in which Bitcoin was divided into equal parts and distributed to Bitcoin holders is Bitcoin Cash.

Uniswap (UNI) Airdrop: Users who had engaged with the platform could obtain UNI tokens through an airdrop offered by the decentralized exchange protocol Uniswap.

Cryptocurrency holders have an exciting way to diversify their portfolios and obtain unexpected benefits through airdrops and forks. It is advisable for participants to remain updated about prospective opportunities, use caution to steer clear of scams, and thoroughly assess the worth and possible consequences of newly obtained assets as a result of airdrops and forks.

C. Engaging in Affiliate Programs: Converting Support into Cryptocurrency Benefits

By using their networks and promoting particular goods or services within the cryptocurrency ecosystem, affiliate programs offer people a flexible way to generate passive income. This strategy entails endorsing platforms, exchanges, or goods associated with cryptocurrencies and rewarding successful referrals with cryptocurrency. Let's examine affiliate programs in more detail and see how users can earn cryptocurrency for their advocacy:

1. Comprehending Affiliate Programs:

Promotional Partnerships: Product or service providers and individuals who serve as affiliates form promotional partnerships through affiliate programs. By bringing new users or customers to the platform, affiliates get paid to promote the goods and services and receive commissions or other incentives.

Tracking Referrals: Usually, affiliates receive special codes or links for referrals. The affiliate gets paid for the referral when users use these links or codes to register, buy something, or interact with the platform.

2. How Cryptocurrency Affiliate Programs Operate:

Exchanges for cryptocurrencies: In order to promote user acquisition, a large number of cryptocurrency exchanges and trading platforms provide affiliate programs. In exchange for introducing users to the platform and encouraging them to sign up and trade, affiliates get paid a commission or a portion of the trading fees.

Wallets and Services: Affiliate programs may be offered by wallet providers, hardware wallet manufacturers, and other cryptocurrency-related services. Affiliates who successfully refer customers to these goods or services are rewarded.

3. Advantages of Taking Part in Affiliate Programs:

Affiliate programs offer a passive income stream to individuals who can effectively leverage their networks and engage in promotional activities.

Diversification of Earnings: Depending on the platforms they choose to promote, participants can earn a variety of cryptocurrencies through affiliate programs, allowing them to diversify their cryptocurrency holdings.

Alignment of Interests: Since the success of their referrals affects their own financial success, affiliates frequently have a stake in promoting high-quality goods or services.

4. Success Techniques:

Targeted Promotion: Affiliates can profit from targeted promotion that targets audiences with an interest in investing in, trading, or particular products related to the cryptocurrency space.

Educative Content: Educating potential referrals about the advantages of the platforms or services being promoted can increase their trust and level of engagement.

Transparent Communication: Giving the audience clear and concise information about the conditions and advantages of the affiliate program promotes credibility and trust.

5. Dangers and Things to Think About:

Reputation of the Platform: Affiliates need to be aware of the standing of the websites or services they endorse. To stay credible, you have to stand with reliable and respectable organizations.

Regulatory Compliance: When it comes to promoting financial goods and services, affiliates must be aware of and abide by all relevant regulations.

6. Cryptocurrency Affiliate Program Examples:

One of the biggest cryptocurrency exchanges, Binance, has an affiliate program through which users can get paid for successfully referring new users to the website.

Ledger Hardware Wallet Affiliate Program: Users can receive incentives for recommending their safe hardware wallets through Ledger's affiliate program.

Engaging in affiliate programs within the cryptocurrency ecosystem enables people to share worthwhile products or services with their networks, monetize their advocacy, and receive compensation in the form of cryptocurrency. Through tactical promotional efforts and a commitment to reliable platforms, players can access a consistent flow of income without investment in the ever-changing cryptocurrency market.

In conclusion

a. Synopsis of Important Ideas: Accepting the Core of Cryptocurrency Understanding

Let's review the main ideas that have emerged as we draw to a close this investigation into the complex world of cryptocurrencies. This thorough guide sought to simplify difficult subjects into easily understood information for novices, giving them a head start in navigating the world of cryptocurrencies:

1. Bitcoin's past:

Pioneering Innovation: The 2009 introduction of Bitcoin by the anonymous Satoshi Nakamoto set the stage for the development of peer-to-peer, decentralized digital currency. It was established in response to the problems with conventional financial systems.

2. Blockchain Technology:

Decentralized Ledger: The blockchain, the underlying technology of cryptocurrencies, is a transparent, tamper-resistant, decentralized ledger. It promotes the dawn of a new era of digital trust by enabling safe and trustless transactions.

3. Frequently Used Cryptocurrencies:

Beyond Bitcoin: Other cryptocurrencies with distinct features and applications, such as Ethereum, Ripple, Litecoin, and others, have broadened the cryptocurrency landscape. Investors can diversify their portfolios by being aware of their differences.

4. Blockchain applications:

Smart Contracts: Smart contracts are programmable, self-executing contracts made possible by blockchain technology, which goes beyond money.

Supply Chain Management: By increasing supply chain traceability and transparency, blockchain lowers fraud and boosts productivity.

Digital Identity: Safe and user-controlled identity verification is possible with decentralized identity solutions on the blockchain.

5. Opportunities for Earnings:

Long-Term Investments: Using dollar-cost averaging, investigating staking, and holding cryptocurrencies as long-term investments all present chances for passive income.

Trading Strategies: The cornerstones of profitable cryptocurrency trading are risk management, trend analysis, and fundamental trading principles.

Staking and mining: Staking is the process of participating in a blockchain network's consensus to earn rewards, while mining is the process of validating transactions.

6. Assets in Cryptocurrencies:

Portfolio diversification is essential for controlling risk and maximizing returns. It is a smart move to spread your investments over a variety of cryptocurrencies and assets.

Risk management: For investments to be successful, it is imperative to recognize and control risks, set stop-loss orders, and keep up with market developments.

7. Other Ways to Make Money:

Airdrops and Forks: These unforeseen events can give cryptocurrency holders access to extra assets by way of airdrops and forks.

Affiliate Programs: By endorsing cryptocurrency platforms and services, members of affiliate programs can generate passive income.

8. Prospects for the Future:

Evolutionary Trends: The world of cryptocurrencies is always changing as a result of innovations like decentralized finance (DeFi), non-fungible tokens (NFTs), and continuous blockchain research.

Regulatory Environment: As the cryptocurrency market matures, regulatory changes have a big impact on investor confidence and market dynamics.

9. Looking Ahead: Managing Cryptocurrencies in the Future

The world of cryptocurrencies promises new opportunities, revolutionary technologies, and ongoing innovation in the future. People can prosper in this innovative and dynamic ecosystem by adopting a mindset of constant learning, following market trends, and adjusting to regulatory changes.

The journey into cryptocurrencies is an endless exploration, regardless of your interest: trading, investing, or just curious about the future of finance. The opportunities and challenges presented by the landscape will also change as it does. I hope that you will approach the world of cryptocurrencies with curiosity, caution, and a goal of financial empowerment.

b. A Brief Glossary of Key Terms: Getting Around the Crypto Lexicon

As our exploration of the world of cryptocurrencies comes to an end, let's quickly create an encyclopedia of the key terms that have been essential to our learning. The purpose of this glossary is to provide a useful guide for understanding the wide-ranging and constantly-changing vocabulary of the cryptocurrency world.

1. Blockchain:

Definition: A technology that records transactions over a network of computers using a decentralized, tamper-resistant ledger. It is the foundation of the majority of cryptocurrencies.

2. Bitcoin:

Definition: Created by Satoshi Nakamoto in 2009, bitcoin is the first and most well-known cryptocurrency. Bitcoin is a peer-to-peer digital currency that runs on a network.

3. Ethereum

Definition: A decentralized platform that makes it possible to develop decentralized apps (DApps) and smart contracts. Its native cryptocurrency is ether (ETH).

4. Alternative Coins:

Any cryptocurrency that isn't Bitcoin, by definition. Ethereum, Ripple, Litecoin, and a myriad of other cryptocurrencies are examples.

5. Intelligent Contracts:

Definition: Contracts that are self-executing and have their terms encoded directly into the code. They use blockchain technology to automate and enforce contracts.

6. Management of the Supply Chain:

Definition: The application of blockchain technology to supply chains to improve traceability and transparency while lowering fraud and increasing efficiency.

7. Online Persona:

Definition: A decentralized method of managing identities through the use of blockchain technology for safe, user-controlled identity verification.

8. Extended-Term Capital:

Definition: Prolonged cryptocurrency holding, frequently motivated by the hope that prices will rise in the long run.

9. Average Dollar-Cost (DCA):

Definition: An approach in which investors, independent of the asset's price, routinely invest a predetermined sum in cryptocurrencies at prearranged intervals.

10. Trading strategies are methods that traders employ in order to make well-informed choices about whether to purchase or sell cryptocurrencies. comprises breakout trading, trend following, and trading at resistance and support.

11. Definition of mining: - Mining is the process of using intricate mathematical calculations to validate transactions before adding them to the blockchain. New cryptocurrency coins are awarded to miners.

12. Staking is the process of locking up a specific quantity of cryptocurrency in order to contribute to the security and validation of a blockchain network. Rewards are earned through staking.

13. Airdrops: - Definition: The giving away of free cryptocurrency tokens or coins to owners of native assets on a particular blockchain.

14. Forks are defined as: - Occurs when a blockchain experiences a major modification that creates two new, independent blockchains.

15. Affiliate programs are defined as promotional alliances in which participants (affiliates) receive payments or incentives in exchange for introducing new clients or users to a product or service.

16. Decentralized Finance (DeFi) is a movement that aims to transform traditional financial services like trading, lending, and borrowing by utilizing decentralized networks.

17. Non-Fungible Tokens (NFTs): - Definition: Distinctive digital assets recorded on the blockchain, frequently signifying possession of digital or tangible objects such as collectibles, music, or artwork.

18. The regulatory landscape, which affects investor confidence and market dynamics, is defined as the constantly changing set of laws governing the use and trading of cryptocurrencies.

This brief encyclopedia provides an overview of the extensive jargon used in the cryptocurrency space. Being aware of these ideas will enable people to handle the opportunities and challenges that lie ahead as the industry develops further.

C. Accept the Journey: An Appeal for Ongoing Cryptocurrency Research

As we draw to a close this in-depth introduction to the world of cryptocurrencies, think of it as a jumping off point for your continued research into this ever-changing and exciting environment. The world of cryptocurrencies is constantly changing, offering countless chances for education, development, and financial empowerment. Here's an incentive to learn more about this intriguing field:

1. Develop Your Curiosity:

Potential Is Unleashed by Curiosity: Approach the cryptocurrency space with an open mind. Develop an inquisitive mind that propels you to comprehend the underlying technologies, market trends, and cutting-edge advancements.

2. Remain Up to Date:

Keep up with the most recent developments, legislative adjustments, and technical breakthroughs in the bitcoin ecosystem. Knowledge truly is power. To learn more, investigate reliable news sites, discussion boards, and learning environments on a regular basis.

3. Make Contact with the Community:

Participate and Learn: Get involved in offline and online cryptocurrency communities. Participate in conversations, pose inquiries, and gain knowledge from the experiences of others. Communities offer priceless insights, a range of viewpoints, and a feeling of contagious enthusiasm.

4. Try Out Some Caution:

Practical Experience: To obtain practical experience, think about conducting small-scale cryptocurrency experiments. Take advantage of this chance to investigate various wallets, trading systems, and financial plans. Learn by doing, but make sure to exercise caution and manage your risks.

5. Investigate Emerging Trends:

Examine cutting-edge concepts like non-fungible tokens (NFTs) and decentralized finance (DeFi). These signify novel opportunities for financial inclusion, creativity, and ownership in the realm of cryptocurrencies.

6. Make connections and work together:

Work Together with Like Minds: Make connections with people who are as passionate about cryptocurrencies as you are. Participate in events, go to meetups, and work together on projects. The bitcoin community is based on cooperation and knowledge sharing.

7. Be Adaptable:

Adapt to Changes: Cryptocurrency markets are dynamic, and the regulatory landscape is ever-changing. Be adaptable and responsive to market trends and regulatory developments. Flexibility is a valuable trait in navigating this evolving space.

8. Educate Others:

Share Your Knowledge: As you deepen your understanding of cryptocurrencies, consider sharing your knowledge with others. Educate friends, family, and peers about the potential benefits and risks, contributing to broader awareness and adoption.

9. Learn from Setbacks:

Resilience in Setbacks: In the world of cryptocurrencies, setbacks and challenges are part of the journey. Embrace them as opportunities for growth and learning. Resilience in the face of adversity is a hallmark of successful participants in this space.

10. Contribute to the Ecosystem: - Contribute to Innovation: Explore ways to contribute to the cryptocurrency ecosystem. Whether through development, research, education, or advocacy, your contributions can play a role in shaping the future of finance.

Remember, the cryptocurrency world is a tapestry of innovation, disruption, and endless possibilities. The more you engage with it, the more you'll uncover its intricacies and potential. Continue your journey with an open mind, a hunger for knowledge, and a willingness to adapt. The future of finance is in motion, and your exploration contributes to the ongoing narrative of this groundbreaking industry. **Happy exploring!**

Additional Resources: Further Reading and Exploration

Congratulations on completing your journey through the world of cryptocurrencies! As you continue to deepen your understanding and explore new horizons in this dynamic field, here are some additional resources to aid you on your quest for knowledge:

Books:

"Mastering Bitcoin" by Andreas M. Antonopoulos

"The Bitcoin Standard: The Decentralized Alternative to Central Banking" by Saifedean Ammous

"Cryptoassets: The Innovative Investor's Guide to Bitcoin and Beyond" by Chris Burniske and Jack Tatar

Online Courses:

Coursera: "Bitcoin and Cryptocurrency Technologies" by Princeton University

Udemy: "Cryptocurrency Investment Course 2022: Fund Your Retirement!" by Suppoman

LinkedIn Learning: "Blockchain Basics" by Jonathan Reichental

Websites and Forums:

CoinDesk: Stay updated with the latest news, analysis, and insights on cryptocurrencies and blockchain technology.

Reddit: Join communities like r/CryptoCurrency and r/Bitcoin for discussions, news, and insights from fellow enthusiasts.

Bitcoin.org: Access beginner-friendly resources, wallet recommendations, and information about Bitcoin.

Podcasts:

"Unchained" by Laura Shin: Dive deep into blockchain and cryptocurrency topics with insightful interviews and discussions.

"The Pomp Podcast" by Anthony Pompliano: Explore the latest trends and developments in the cryptocurrency space with industry experts.

YouTube Channels:

Andreas M. Antonopoulos: Gain insights into Bitcoin, blockchain, and decentralized technologies from one of the industry's most respected voices.

DataDash: Explore cryptocurrency trading strategies, market analysis, and investment insights with Nicholas Merten.

Social Media:

Twitter: Follow thought leaders, developers, and influencers in the cryptocurrency space for real-time updates and discussions.

LinkedIn: Join cryptocurrency and blockchain-related groups to network with professionals and stay informed about industry trends.

Meetups and Events:

Meetup.com: Attend local cryptocurrency and blockchain meetups to connect with like-minded individuals and participate in discussions and workshops.

Conferences: Keep an eye out for cryptocurrency and blockchain conferences and events in your area or attend virtual events to learn from industry experts and thought leaders.

Remember to approach additional resources with a critical mindset, verifying information from multiple sources and staying cautious of potential scams or misinformation. Your continued exploration and engagement in the cryptocurrency world will contribute to your growth and understanding of this exciting and transformative industry. Happy learning!

www.ingramcontent.com/pod-product-compliance
Lightning Source LLC
Chambersburg PA
CBHW060108300526
45791CB00018B/503